The Heart Space

Living with Grace and Ease in an Era of Uncertainty

CHRISTINE SAMUEL

INNER WORK PRESS

© 2024 by Christine Samuel

All rights reserved.

No part of this publication may be reproduced, distributed, or transmitted in any form or by any means, including photocopying, recording, or other electronic or mechanical methods, without the prior written permission of the author, except in the case of brief quotations embodied in critical reviews and certain other non-commercial uses permitted by copyright law.

This book presents the author's subjective insights and is intended for informational purposes only. It does not replace professional healthcare or mental health advice. Neither the author nor the publisher can be held responsible for how this information is used. It is strongly advised to consult a qualified healthcare or mental health professional for decisions regarding your own or others' health.

ISBN

978-1-7381988-2-5 (E-book)

978-1-7381988-0-1 (Paperback)

978-1-7381988-3-2 (Hardcover)

Published by Inner Work Press, Toronto, Canada

For permission requests or inquiries, please contact the author at christine@christinesamuel.ca.

For more information about the author and the book, visit www.christine-samuel.ca.

*For my husband and children–Robertson, Samuel, and Naomi.
Thank you for being you.*

*Dedicated to humanity and our cherished planet.
Welcome to the Era of the Heart.*

Nothing in life is to be feared, it is only to be understood. Now is the time to understand more, so that we may fear less.

MARIE CURIE

INTRODUCTION

If this book has found its way into your hands, chances are you've felt a whisper of something more profound in life. Perhaps you're on a quest for a deeper purpose and longing for true fulfillment or yearn to make a significant impact and discover a new way of being in this changing world.

But it is hard, isn't it? Our brains are wired to seek predictability, creating tension between our desire for control and our openness to new possibilities.

When we find ourselves at a crossroad between the old and new, embracing the unknown is one of the most challenging things to do. Our fears and resistance magnify in these moments. As a result, we often doubt ourselves, with a persistent question looming in the background:

Am I doing the right thing?

I intimately understand this struggle. After enduring a year of toxic work culture, I made the bold decision to step away from my corporate career of over 20 years. I asked myself: If not now, when? If not you, who?

I yearned to live a different kind of life—one driven by joy, purpose, and the freedom to be.

But, oh boy! The more I yearned for freedom, the more I had to confront fear. Fear of the unknown, fear of not having enough money, fear of failure, fear of making a wrong move. I realized that fear and scarcity are the primary driving forces in our lives. We've been conditioned to believe that there is never enough—never enough time, money, success, or progress. This incessant desire for more creates a strong need for control, infiltrating every aspect of our lives and leaving us with an insatiable longing for certainty in an unpredictable world.

As a result, I grappled with two fundamental questions: What do you do when you realize the path you've taken no longer serves you? How can you find solid footing when navigating the turbulent waters of transition?

These inquiries have led me to a profound discovery—one that I am excited to share with you in this book. Through my own experience and in guiding others on their journey, I have come to believe:

- Navigating uncertainty calls for a whole new way of knowing.
- Creating deep connections with ourselves and others demands a different kind of listening.
- Cultivating a fresh perspective requires us to find a new way of relating to the world.
- And if we genuinely want to create a better world, we must fundamentally shift our way of being.

Achieving these objectives requires nurturing a steadfast

inner trust and sense of safety that aren't contingent on external circumstances. The Heart Space is the most fertile ground for nurturing these qualities.

This book encourages you to look within and discover a deeper understanding of yourself. It invites you to embrace the paradoxes of life and acknowledge that while everything may change, something inside you remains constant and unchanging. This newfound awareness can make you feel safe within, enabling you to move forward with peace of mind, even when your path ahead is unclear.

It offers guidance to expand your heart and create a sanctuary capable of embracing the complexities that make you who you are. Only when you fully accept and love yourself, with all imperfections and nuances, can you navigate the world's complexities and ambiguities with love and understanding. This gift of self-acceptance leads to greater resilience and adaptability in the face of challenges and uncertainties.

Join me as I share experiences, practices, and the valuable lessons I've gained from guiding numerous individuals through their unique transitions. I wholeheartedly encourage you to dive into this book and uncover the magic held within its pages.

WHAT TO EXPECT

To provide greater clarity, I've organized the book into two sections. The Head Space comprises Chapters 1-4, while The Heart Space includes Chapters 5-10. This way, you can recognize their differences and understand how they play their parts in your experience. Each chapter also contains thought-provoking questions to help you uncover simple truths in your life.

Towards the end of the book, you can immerse yourself in the qualities of the Heart Space through experiential practices. These practices will increase your heart's receptivity and allow your innermost self to be known. Thus, making decisions from a place of love, wisdom, compassion, and clarity becomes easier.

SECTION 1: HEAD SPACE

The initial section delves into the inner workings of the mind, uncovering the roots of fears while revealing a fundamental truth: the boundaries and divisions we perceive around us are the products of our thinking. It contends that life cannot be understood and experienced by thinking alone. In fact, the cause of our dissatisfaction and suffering lies in our way of thinking. The way we use our minds has reduced our ability to fully experience life and express what we are capable of as human beings.

The suffering I refer to here is not the physical deprivation of basic needs. Instead, it is our mental and emotional suffering—such as anxiety, stress, depression, guilt, shame, worry, fear, frustration, and more. This type of suffering does not see your social status, race, religion, education, gender, or geographical location. It affects every human on this planet, and it has been heightened in the era of hyper-connectivity and social media, where distractions increasingly match the speed of our time-traveled mind.

It goes to a thought-provoking exploration of how our thinking and analytical minds are primarily designed for survival, capable of conjuring the worst possible scenarios through their own logic. This inclination can turn our reasoning and analysis into tools for control, fixating on perceived deficiencies as a means for self-protection and gaining a sense of security.

Without trust, love, or connection, our autopilot function relies on fear to keep us safe, holding us in a pattern of control and survival. Even our insatiable desire for growth and success is mostly driven by the underlying belief of not having enough. It's time to break free from these patterns and embrace living from the Heart Space.

SECTION 2: HEART SPACE

In the second half of this book, I will show you how living from the Heart Space makes life easier. When we live from it, doing becomes effortless, thinking hard becomes unnecessary, and peace of mind comes naturally.

By tapping into the nature of the heart, you expand your capacity to hold contradictions and discomfort. Instead of rushing for quick answers, you learn the art of sitting with opposing ideas, perspectives, and emotions. This practice opens the door to new insights and resolutions.

In truth, life is more than just solving problems, erasing differences, or maintaining a status quo. Its divine purpose is to facilitate our personal and collective growth. When we can hold contradictions, even for just a moment, and embrace their existence, we open the possibility for solutions to present themselves.

The Heart Space is filled with wonder, empathy, compassion, love, connection, and intuition. It provides a larger container than the Head Space to handle fear and discomfort. When you tap into these qualities, you open yourself up to new possibilities and ways of being. From here, your life transforms; it suddenly feels like you are enough and whole. You recognize the interconnected web of life that supports you, and that you're part of something much greater. This deeper understanding brings a strong sense of ease and peace. As a result, you find the freedom to move and be in this world just as you are. And when you can simply be who you are, you become one with the flow of life.

These transformative insights and experiences await you within the chapters dedicated to the Heart Space.

To better understand what this book offers, I've compiled some feedback from the women who participated in my "Moving from Head to Heart Mastery" program, which covered the same practices and principles found in this book.

Here are their thoughts:

> I am more comfortable within myself and willing to take the courage to honor uncomfortable feelings and emotions as they are happening to free them and learn. Time with Christine has opened myself to me. I feel more confident about finding ways forward and not staying stuck in feelings of despair and hopelessness. I am gaining an understanding and awareness of the difference between choosing from my head and choosing from my heart. I am beginning a new year with confidence instead of fear. I am learning to be more comfortable with uncertainty.
>
> KATHY G.

It has helped me see how, when I get "out of my head" and come from a more "feeling" sense, my heart, I "feel" more grounded and centered. It has helped me understand how limited the possibilities and perspectives can be when we are just guided by our minds/our thoughts. Listening to my heart "feeling" what is resonating inside me has helped create so much more openness and an expansive lens through which I can see and feel.

BARB L.

I have much more clarity with decision-making now. I am no longer wobbling between my head and what I think other people want. I am living from my heart.

LAURIN M.

I have become more open and softer around some things that are important to me. I'm learning to "softly hold" strongly held opinions and beliefs without compulsion.

ANITA W.

I encourage you to read this book with your mind and heart wide open. Instead of striving to grasp it, create space and allow your inner wisdom to speak to you through the book. Listen to what feels true within yourself as you read.

Every chapter in this book is written to provide new insights each time you return to it. Understanding has no limit. As you grow within yourself, it will grow with you.

Are you ready to start?

SECTION ONE: THE HEAD SPACE

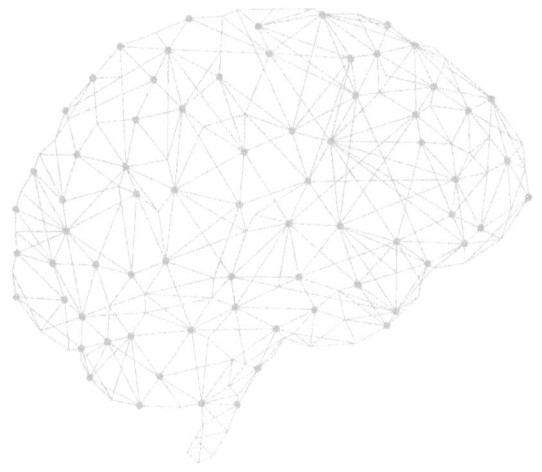

ONE
THE KNIFE WE USE

We cannot solve our problems with the same thinking we used when we created them.

ALBERT EINSTEIN

Everything–including people, objects, and ideas–has its own special qualities. Have you ever considered the natural tendencies of your thinking?

Imagine a world where the knife had never been invented. Life moved at a slower pace. People relied on their bare hands, rocks, or even their teeth to break objects into rough shapes. Then, one extraordinary day, a wizard from another world appeared, bestowing a magical tool for precise cutting. "Knife" was its name. With a simple motion, objects could be cut into two. The wizard taught the people to make knives, and in time, they extended this principle to make scissors, saws, and axes.

This tool revolutionized their lives and society. Cooking

and food preparation evolved, ushering in a new era of culinary artistry. The style of furniture transformed with precise cuts and shapes. Preparing food and cutting wood became faster and more efficient.

Soon, everyone owned a knife. Many people even had several in assorted sizes. Recognizing its cutting prowess, they began teaching their children to wield knives. Over time, they extrapolated the knife's usefulness beyond cutting and incorporated the tool into various aspects of daily life, including writing, playing, resting, sleeping, and working. Knives became an indispensable part of their routines.

However, a peculiar phenomenon began to afflict every town, north and south, east and west, wherever you could find humans. Chronic skin bleeding afflicted people of all ages. Some had it in their mouths, while others had it on their fingers, arms, necks, backs, and feet. Even though the wounds would heal, they always reappeared elsewhere on their bodies.

The society's intellectuals gathered to solve this mysterious affliction. Pharmacists devised a powerful anti-pain medication, while scientists developed artificial skin replacement methods. Dietitians recommended a reduced eating frequency to control symptoms. Inventors and designers created materials to protect the skin. The economy, healthcare, technology, and education sectors evolved around the widespread skin bleeding.

Ironically, they were unaware that the excessive bleeding was caused by their use of the knife for *everything*—far beyond its intended purpose.

This story *is* absurd, and you might find it ridiculous that people failed to notice the obvious cause of their problem! But before you judge too harshly, consider that the people in this tale are not so different from us.

We, too, use knives for everything—not the knife you and I are familiar with—but the knife of our thinking. Let me explain.

In the realm of the Head Space, our thinking knives carry great significance, exemplifying the sharpness of our logic and intellect. They serve as tools that enable us to break things down into smaller pieces so we can comprehend and analyze the world.

As Peter Hawkins, a Professor of Leadership at Henley Business School, says:

> To make sense of the world, we apply the analytic scissors and create cuts in the seamless web of life, but we then forget that it is our own thinking that has created the cuts and the boundaries, and we think the cuts and boundaries exist 'out-there' in the world.

Since the Scientific Revolution in the 16th century, the precision of our analytical and intellectual abilities has propelled us into the fastest-growing era of science and technology in human history. We have benefited from it. Innovations in science and technology have increased the average human lifespan and brought access to information we now cannot live without.

From the age of five to their twenties, we send our children to school to learn and develop their intellectual minds. Those with brilliant intellect often receive more power and larger financial rewards.

Thinking has become a sign of our existence, and we don't

know what to do without it. Living involves continually analyzing and forming opinions about ourselves and the world around us. We don't even realize the deductive nature of our analytical mind because it is so ingrained in us. While René Descartes famously proclaimed, "I think, therefore I am," the impact of thinking goes far beyond mere existence. It permeates every aspect of our being, influencing our self-worth and happiness.

Moreover, our tendency to compartmentalize various aspects of our lives makes this fragmentation worse. We separate our professional lives from our personal lives, our passions from our jobs, our minds from our bodies, our feelings from our thoughts, our spiritual lives from our daily lives, and our economy from its environmental impact. As Sufi mystic Kabir Helminski puts it, "We sustain ourselves in the state of defragmentation to the extent that we feel lonely, alienated, incomplete, and in conflict with ourselves."

THE RISE OF THE ANALYTICAL MIND

As far as the written records go, analytical thinking has a long history that goes back to the ancient Greek philosopher Socrates. However, it wasn't until the birth of the Scientific Revolution in the 16th century that this type of thinking began to take off. Scientists and philosophers such as Copernicus, Kepler, Sir Francis Bacon, Galileo Galilei, René Descartes, and Sir Isaac Newton played significant roles in shaping our understanding of nature and reality.

These individuals could measure and understand the world like never before by using advances in mathematics, physics, astronomy, biology, human anatomy, and chemistry.

They showed that nature and the universe are mechanical and can be analyzed and explained in mechanistic terms. This led to the idea that nature can be treated as an external, objectified entity to be studied and manipulated for our benefit.

THE SEPARATION OF HUMANS FROM NATURE

Sir Francis Bacon (1561–1626), an English philosopher and political leader widely recognized as the mastermind behind the Scientific Revolution, introduced a new philosophy that radically altered the relationship between humans and nature. He championed an inductive method of acquiring knowledge by testing and refining hypotheses through observation, experimentation, and isolating outside factors to control variables. This approach allowed for more objective and universal knowledge; what Bacon called a "machine for thinking." He believed it would guide humanity to an understanding of the natural world.

Bacon believed that by increasing knowledge through experimentation, humans could extend their dominion over nature. He viewed nature as a female entity withholding her secrets, who would only yield them to a man who dominated her. Bacon famously wrote, "Nature must be taken by the forelock" (grabbed by her hair). It was necessary to subdue her, to shake her to her foundations so that man could thrive.

Through Bacon's mechanistic view, nature is reduced to mere matter. Thus, nature quickly became commodified to benefit the human economy and industry. The separation of humans from nature, which led to scientific and technological innovations, came at a high price. It is still happening today. As we become more disconnected from nature, we see more environmental destruction and climate change have accelerated at a rapid rate.

As David Suzuki, an environmental activist, once said,

> The way we see the world shapes the way we treat it. If a mountain is a deity, not a pile of ore; if a river is one of the veins of the land, not potential irrigation water; if a forest is a sacred grove, not timber; if other species are biological kin, not resources; or if the planet is our mother, not an opportunity—then we will treat each other with greater respect. This is the challenge, to look at the world from a different perspective.

Suzuki's alternative perspective embodies a timeless wisdom that has gradually faded since the dawn of the Scientific Revolution.

THE SEPARATION OF MIND FROM BODY

The division between humans and nature soon became even wider at the individual level.

Let's visit Leiden, Netherlands in 1640, where the illustrious mathematician and philosopher René Descartes took pen to paper in a desperate quest for certainty and a solid foundation of knowledge. Plagued by doubt, he arrived at the iconic declaration: *"Cogito, ergo sum"* ("I think, therefore I am."). Descartes reasoned that the mind and thinking were distinct from the physical body because our senses were untrustworthy and easily deceived. Yet, he could never question the existence of his own thoughts. He decided that true knowledge could only be reached through pure intellectual perception.

In the 16th and 17th centuries, specialization took root in Western civilizations. Mind and spirit belonged to the business of religion, while nature and the mechanics of things belonged to the business of science. Such specialization enabled modern colonialism to flourish. Industry and commerce, backed by mechanistic science and innovation, could exploit natural resources and institute the slavery of Indigenous populations without needing to check in with their conscience. The church, which held its cross on the pulse of the mind and body of its parishioners, saw no wrongdoing in these acts. Instead, it sought to "save" the new batch of souls brought to it by systemic colonialization.

DISCONNECTION FROM ALIVENESS

As we fragment the mind from the body in our search for logical reasoning and explanations, we inadvertently detach ourselves from our embodied senses. We perceive the world and our experiences as separate objects, distant from our very being. Our thoughts and conversations revolve around opinions and judgments, leaving little space for genuine immersion in the present moment. This process of slicing and compartmentalizing our experiences through analytical thinking impedes our ability to grasp the subtle signals emanating from our bodies.

Once integral to our being, our feelings are now treated like objects. We see them as external commodities obtained through accomplishments or actions. On the other hand, we push away "negative" emotions like anxiety or boredom. The natural feeling of being alive and vibrant becomes something far away, only reachable if we keep working hard.

As a result, life takes on a mechanical and calculated quality. We believe true happiness resides in some future state, contingent upon acquiring specific outcomes. We forget that happiness resides within us, requiring no prerequisites or complex formulas.

If we observe children at play, we will witness their ability to tap into their innate joy and contentment. They remind us that happiness is our birthright, inherent in our nature.

But you may argue, "Yeah, it's easy for children to be joyful; they don't have to pay their bills and mortgage."

There!

This statement shows our tendency to construct and conceptualize some prerequisites for happiness—adding complexity and attaching specific conditions needed to attain our desired emotional state. Doing things simply because they bring joy is never enough inside the hypothetical and calculative mind.

Our constant pursuit of future happiness brings about angst and anxiety that permeate every aspect of our lives. We struggle to focus on the task at hand because our minds are preoccupied with worrying about what comes next. We find it challenging to be present with our loved ones because our thoughts are consumed by what needs to be done. We become slaves to our incessant analytical thinking, which exhausts our bodies and keeps us awake at night.

As Alan Watts warns in *The Wisdom of Insecurity*:

> Since what we know of the future is made up of purely abstract and logical elements—inferences, guesses, deduc-

tions—it cannot be eaten, felt, smelled, seen, heard, or otherwise enjoyed. To pursue it is to pursue a constantly retreating phantom, and the faster you chase it, the faster it runs ahead.

Our thinking can point to our experience, but it is not the experience itself. There is a difference between the felt-sense experience and an idea about it. For instance, having extensive knowledge of Kyoto through reading or watching videos cannot replicate the firsthand experience of being physically present and experiencing the city yourself.

The language of the mind resides within the realm of concepts, ideas, and meanings. While valuable, it falls short of encompassing the entirety of reality. Just as Bruce Lee cautions his student in the movie *Enter the Dragon*, "It is like a finger pointing away to the moon. Don't concentrate on the finger; you will miss all that heavenly glory."

For the same reason, the concept of empathy is not the same as *empathy*. An idea about God is not the same as *God*. The intellectual definition of Love is not *Love* itself. The only way to understand is to fully immerse yourself in the experience. So, if we seek to comprehend Love, we must become Love. This holistic understanding cannot be obtained solely through our Head Space. Thinking alone cannot grant us the intimacy and aliveness found within experience.

Furthermore, our ability to connect with others diminishes when we lose touch with our own aliveness. Instead of truly listening and understanding other people's perspective, we rush to form opinions and craft our responses before they finish speaking. How can we be present when we habitually interpret, analyze, and hold opinions about everything, including our thoughts and feelings?

Being present, once a natural capacity of every living being, has become a skill that must be learned through mindfulness and meditation. While many books and methods are available, people often struggle to grasp its essence. To truly understand *being present*, you must embody it.

The cut we make to extract our experience into intellectual abstraction makes us lose touch with the rawness and vitality of life. We become like spectators, standing apart from the existence we are meant to fully embrace. The moment becomes a means to an end, an item to check off our to-do list, rather than a precious gift to cherish.

THE COST OF RIGIDITY

Our predominant reliance on analytical thinking has resulted in excessive fragmentation, leading to rigidity in our perception of ourselves and the world.

Moshé Feldenkrais, the pioneer of the Somatic movement, observed how specialization in modern life leads to rigidity and dysfunction. In his work, *Body and Mature Behavior*, he notes, "The use they make of their eyes adapts them most perfectly to that particular use only but renders them almost useless for other purposes." He explained that when individuals suppress certain activities, they become rigid. He emphasized that continuously adhering to any principle, regardless of its quality, results in the ongoing suppression of certain functions.

From a physiological standpoint, the impact is evident. Our modern lifestyles entail extensive time gazing at screens, maintaining prolonged sitting positions, and leading sedentary lives. Consequently, our bodies' flexibility and mobility diminish, often resulting in neck and back tightness. Moreover, excessive fixation on smartphones and laptop screens limits peripheral vision and reduces our awareness of the surrounding environment.

Drawing a parallel, relying exclusively on our analytical prowess can decrease our mental and emotional agility, impairing our capacity to perceive a bigger picture and adopt a broader perspective. This decline in capability doesn't originate from external factors. It happens when we underutilize other faculties, such as intuition, creativity, and multi-sensory abilities. This aligns with the saying, "Use it or lose it," which illustrates the concept of brain neuroplasticity.

Just like an actual knife, our thinking knife is inherently neutral. Its goodness and usefulness depend on how we use it. Let's acknowledge its purpose and understand that analytical thinking is just one tool in our vast mental toolbox.

To thrive, we should expand our awareness and adopt a balanced approach, integrating intuition, creativity, and being present with our experiences. This integration allows us to navigate life's intricacies and gain greater wisdom. It frees us from the constraints of relying solely on our thinking knife.

REFLECTIONS AT YOUR OWN PACE

1. Reflect on moments when you feel disconnected from your body or the natural world. What triggers these instances, and what can you do to foster a deeper sense of connection and aliveness?

2. In the story of the knife, the people became heavily reliant on the tool, leading to unintended consequences. Can you draw parallels between their over reliance on the knife and your own tendency towards analysis paralysis? How might excessive analysis and overthinking limit your ability to take action and make progress?

TWO
LIVING IN THE MIND-MADE WORLD

The mind alone is the creator of the world.

RISHI VASISTHA

Have you ever seen an image or video of Earth from outer space? It's a beautiful sight, isn't it? A blue and green planet covered by gracefully moving white clouds. If you look closely, you can see the lines that mark the edges between the land and the ocean on the surface of the perfectly round Earth. But can you find the lines between countries?

Country borders do not exist on Earth; they only appear on the maps and globes crafted by humans. They are a mind-made concept widely accepted as reality. Yet, these imaginary lines have impacted billions of people, shaped history and even led to wars and the loss of lives in their defense.

The same lines that delineate countries have become the center of human activities, economy, politics, and resources.

In fact, infrastructure and governance have been created to support the idea of a country, dictating who can enter, who cannot, and how to manage it all.

Isn't a passport mind-made? Only humans must have a passport for exiting and entering a country, while birds, fish, insects, and other animals can fly and roam as they please. The idea of a passport has led to the creation of thousands, if not millions, of jobs worldwide to manage immigration. Additionally, border control has led to the emergence of new categories for humans, such as immigrants, aliens, and refugees—all determined by who can enter or exit our artificially delineated territories. It's fascinating how this small piece of paper can have such far-reaching implications in our society.

This is just a simple example of our intricate, interconnected mind-made system. Our lives are at the center of this system, living in and fueling the mind-made world.

Take a moment to consider how many of your struggles, conflicts, efforts, and challenges arise from attempting to conform to the constructs of the mind-made world.

Even *success* is a mind-made idea.

The Latin word for success, *successus*, means "a good result or happy outcome." Its modern meaning, related to achieving a desired goal, evolved during the Scientific Revolution. The concept of success as a measure of personal or organizational accomplishment gained significant attention and documentation during the late 19th century. This shift in the meaning of success has had massive consequences.

To succeed in today's mind-made world, you must navigate the complex and multi-layered systems humans have created. Whether you work as a stockbroker, real estate agent, lawyer, accountant, or CEO, your role exists only within this mind-made system. This system governs your daily life far more than natural phenomena like the weather or seasons do. Who decided that your time belongs to your employer or client during certain hours of the day? Who created the rule that you can only take two to six weeks of vacation annually? These restrictions seem normal, but at some point, at some time, society simply made them up!

To further this point, you were educated for the first twenty-plus years of your life to prepare for employment and to fit into our society. You were told that through a chosen career or entrepreneurial track, you could accomplish a desired end and reach a state of prosperity and fulfillment. Yet, it is perplexing how rarely anyone questions the validity of this mind-made track for success.

We all delegate some of our authority and autonomy to a mind-made entity known as the government to handle civil matters. In return for this, we pay taxes, and if we're fortunate enough to live in a country with a well-designed healthcare system, the government supplies healthcare services and infrastructure to us at no additional cost. As you mature and succeed in navigating the financial system, you may enter another mind-made game called property ownership. This illusory process entails determining a sum of money that you are willing to trade for a house, often with many zeroes. Subsequently, that magic number gets exchanged from one mind-made institution to another for some inexplicable reason. Your reward? You must now devote a huge portion of your lifetime to pay for it.

During your productive years, you must ensure you can retire well. Rather than being able to do what you want now, you wait until you have saved enough money for retirement to do what you've always dreamed about.

You see, retirement doesn't exist in nature. A bird never retires. It lives until its last breath.

So why aren't you truly living? Nobody force you to wait until the end of your life to achieve your dreams. There is no guarantee that you'll be around to enjoy them later. Waiting to live out your purpose and passions is a mind-made idea that society perpetuates.

This is a macro-level view of the mind-made world we live in. It originated in the minds of one or more humans, became widely accepted, and evolved into a complex system manifested in the human-made infrastructures and objects we use daily. These systems have been passed down from generation to generation, becoming deeply ingrained into a way of life that we no longer question. They seem as natural as the sun rising in the east and setting in the west. But there is nothing natural about it.

THE REALITY THAT WE LIVE IN IS A MIND-MADE REALITY

When we were born, we relied entirely on bodily sensations to understand the world around us. We felt everything. If hunger struck, we cried. If wetness touched our bottoms, we cried. When warmth and comfort enveloped us, we felt calm and cooed. Fatigue prompted us to sleep, and the sound of a funny voice or sight of a familiar face made us smile and laugh.

When we cried, our mothers provided the food we needed. This simple cause-and-effect relationship was among our earliest lessons. We also discovered that when we wanted something, making a sound was our way to communicate. Different sounds had distinct meanings. As we grew up, we might have associated "Mama" with our mothers and "Dada" with our fathers. We knew that "no" was a magical word to express our reluctance to comply with grown-up requests.

In those early years of development, we learned associations. We understood that a letter had a name and represented a sound. Specific combinations of letters had different sounds and formed words. Each word stood for a particular meaning or object. When we grasped the meaning of a word, we formed mental images of the object it described. Some words even evoked emotions. For instance, the letters h-o-u-s-e represented the word "house." When we thought of a "house," our brains associated it with a building where people or a family lived. We might have even imagined a house of a specific color or shape. These were all associations we learned to make as children.

We also learned specificity. Not all women are your mother. Your mom was not my mom. My dad was not your dad. Your house was not my house. We learned that the building around the corner was not a house but a convenience store.

As we grow older, with our basic associations and specificities in place, our relational associations become even more intricate. Our experiences with our parents can influence how we perceive love and relationships. Your idea of love may differ from mine. Ideas of safety, happiness, and humor vary from person to person.

Even objects take on intricate meanings. How I feel about books cannot be described in a Wikipedia article. No, it stems from past experiences and interactions with books. The shape, texture, and scent of a freshly printed book evoke unique sentiments for me, distinct from those experienced by you or anyone else.

For the most part, our subconscious mind takes over complex associations, making them appear seamless to our conscious mind. We perceive reality as a complex process of associating symbols and meanings. Even when we see a real house, the thoughts or words associated with it aren't the actual house; instead, they are mental concepts shaped by our past experiences and understanding of what a "house" is. In other words, what is in our mind is not the physical house itself but a mental representation of it.

In his book *Deviate: The Science of Seeing Differently*, neuroscientist Beau Lotto argues that human beings do not have access to an accurate perception of reality. Instead, our brain constructs the images we see from the information it already possesses.

Similarly, neuroscientist Anil Seth, who focuses on human perception and consciousness, explains in his essay *The Real Problem* that "what we see, hear, and feel is nothing more than the brain's best guesses of the causes of its sensory inputs." According to Seth, the brain is confined within the skull and has never directly experienced the external world. It relies on the signals it receives from the sensory system, associates them with prior experiences and beliefs about how the world is, and creates the best hypotheses. Therefore, what seems to be occurring outside is happening inside our mind. Our experiences come from the inside out, not from the outside in.

You can have a "house" in your mind when you're

standing in front of one, but you can also have the same house in your mind when you are on vacation, sitting on the beach and staring off into the sunset. Thinking does not have a physical limit, nor is it bounded by time. It exists in the realm of imagination, ideas, and perception. According to Dr. Srini Pillay, a psychiatrist and brain researcher, research suggests that "the circuit that codes for the past overlaps with the circuit that codes for the present and future" in the brain, showing that our perception of time is not cleanly divided into distinct zones.

The complexity of the human mind is fascinating and mind-boggling, no doubt about it. The question is, what does this imply? It means that we don't experience reality; we are experiencing our perception of reality—a construct we create through meaning-making and associations, which is many layers removed from reality.

Let me explain.

Rather than being with what *is*, we respond to our self-created *story* about what is. It may seem that external events—such as the words someone speaks, the news we hear, or the challenging situations we face—trigger our reactions. The truth is that our responses are driven by something alive within us, filled with meaning and emotions.

For instance, picture a scenario where someone's words challenge your deeply held beliefs; the emotional intensity you experience arises from the meaning you ascribe to their words. The more it relates to your identity, needs, survival, values, and what matters to you, the stronger it affects you.

Let's take our understanding a step further and explore how our mental perceptions are similar to how we see objects in the physical world. Imagine you're looking at a massive,

50-story building. If you're standing 30 kilometers (about 18.6 miles) away, it might appear as tiny as your fingertip. However, if you are standing right in front of it and looking up, it will dominate your entire field of vision. What's captivating is that, despite the building's consistent size, your perception of its magnitude alters depending on your position and viewpoint.

It's easy to forget that, as an observer, you are an active participant in the act of looking. Your unique background, past experiences, and individual cognitive and sensory inputs make up what you see and how you interact with the world. Just as you point a camera at something and look through the screen, what you see is no longer the original object, but rather millions of pixels, each with varying degrees of RGB color spectrums. Yet, your brain's remarkable ability to identify patterns and assign meaning fills in the gaps so that you perceive the image on the screen as if it were the original object itself.

The continuous interplay between your perception and response propels you through life. Even the people in your life—your parents, spouse, children, siblings, clients, and coworkers—exist as stories in your mind. How you perceive them shapes how you react and influences your relationships with them. All along, you are dealing with yourself. The actions and words of others serve as a window into your self-perception. As the architect of your own reality, you cannot escape what you have constructed.

POWERFUL BEYOND MEASURE

What is the implication of all of this?

Well, it becomes evident that the world you see isn't an objective reality but a creation of your mind. Your perception shapes your reality. When you view the world as unsafe, you tend to quickly notice potential threats, which can lead to anxiety. But, if you choose to see the world as a friendly and beautiful place, you will see kindness and beauty all around you and feel at peace. You can shape your reality by consciously tapping into your ability to create meaning and connections.

Marianne Williamson famously writes, "Our deepest fear is not that we are inadequate. Our deepest fear is that we are powerful beyond measure." It's important to recognize that we are not mere victims of our circumstances. Our perceptions and thoughts influence how we experience and respond to the world around us.

While the outside world may limit your freedom to speak, move, or belong, no one can take away your freedom to perceive and think as you wish. Our thoughts and perceptions have the power to create something out of nothing and shape our reality. Ironically, while our ability to think and form perception makes us the creators of our own world, we often let it run on autopilot.

As human beings, we have immense power within us. We are the conduits, the alchemists, the living vessels in which perceptions and ideas arise and dissipate. Yes, we can choose to pay attention to one thought over another; we can view the world from multiple perspectives. But do you know we can also step back and observe our thoughts and perceptions with detachment? Developing this capacity allows us to navigate the world with intent and create a reality that aligns with our deepest desires and aspirations.

THE LIMITATIONS OF "I THINK, THEREFORE, I AM"

Let's go back to the philosopher René Descartes, the man who shook humanity upside down and inside out. We have taken his famous statement, "I think, therefore I am," a little too far. Thinking is the doing of being human. However, relying solely on our thoughts to prove our existence can be problematic. Thoughts are constantly changing and unreliable indicators of reality, making it overwhelming and ultimately pointless to keep up with them.

Our modern society places a pervasive expectation on us to engage in thinking and forming opinions on every conceivable issue. It's as if our existence depends on having something to add to a conversation. We often feel we must prove ourselves and show that we're relevant.

As a result, our incessant need to prove our worth turns us into human doings. To feel alive, worthy, growing, and successful in this world, we must prove we are good parents, deserving of a promotion, worthy of love, or excellent leaders. Our self-worth and value go up and down like a yo-yo. Dr. David Hawkins' fishbowl analogy is a powerful metaphor for understanding our thoughts and self-perception. He compares the water in the bowl to our real selves, while our thoughts are like goldfish swimming within it. Sadly, many people mistake themselves for the goldfish.

"I am this regret, I am this worry, I am this failure, I am the one nobody likes."

When we have happy thoughts, we feel so joyful. When we have worrying thoughts, we feel worried. When we think we are failures, we feel bad. Consequently, we try to distract ourselves and use reasoning to produce other thoughts to eliminate the bad feeling and prove that we are not failures. We can experience burnout simply by having our thoughts run amok, especially when we identify ourselves *as* those thoughts.

While thinking is a remarkable human ability, relying too heavily on it as a sign of our existence and who we are, can be limiting and exhausting.

ROOM FOR DIFFERENCES

When we see our thoughts as proof of our existence, their influence extends beyond individuals to society as a whole. Let's dive into a story that illustrates this idea:

Once upon a time, two blind gods lived with a giant elephant so massive that its size and shape spanned the entire universe. The first god had spent his whole life standing in front of the elephant, experiencing its trunk, face, and ears. The second god had spent his life on the back of the elephant, touching and experiencing the tail, the back feet, and the elephant's bump.

One day, the two gods met on Earth, and they felt each other's hearts. They sensed they had something in common: a relationship with the beloved elephant. They decided to speak on a human level, just as humans do, about their experiences living with the elephant.

They talked about the form of the elephant they knew. One god described the elephant as full of big, long cylindrical shapes that could reach him, touch him, and walk forward. The other god said the elephant didn't have any long cylindrical shapes; instead, it had a thin cylinder, stood on two feet, and walked backward.

From that day to eternity, they left their beloved elephant and fought over who was right about the true form of their treasured creature.

We have become like those gods. When your beliefs and opinions—formed through your thinking, perception, culture, and religion—define your identity, what would happen if someone doesn't have the same beliefs and opinions as you?

You and I have both experienced the negative effects of this phenomenon—in friendships, marriages, families, organizations, and communities. Even countries that have fought for their independence can fall apart because of differences in political philosophy. The divisions in our society have never seemed more poignant.

When you hold a different opinion than I do, that means you are wrong, and I am right! When you think I am wrong, I'll make sure I prove that I am right!

We spend so much energy defending and protecting our mental existence at the cost of losing peace and connection with one another. Why? And why do we not see that there is another way?

As long as we reside in a human body, we are bound by the constraints of our mind and language. These limitations are inherently selective, reductive, and restrictive. When we share our thoughts, it is important to remember that our words are not the objective truth but our subjective interpretation of it.

For example, when you describe an elephant, your words do not become the elephant or the absolute truth of the creature. Instead, they help others understand what the elephant looks like from your perspective. When your description differs from mine, it doesn't mean I am wrong. If we don't agree with each other, it doesn't mean I am less or more than you. We are simply seeing things from different angles.

In fact, our differing opinions and perspectives allow us to see a more comprehensive picture of reality, like pieces of a puzzle that come together to form a complete image. Each perspective adds a unique facet to our understanding of the subject. We can arrive at a more holistic and nuanced understanding by sharing and considering different viewpoints. In this way, the diversity of our thoughts and experiences can be seen as an asset rather than a source of conflict.

RESTORING THE ORDER

While living in our Head Space, we often carry a heavy load of thoughts that weighs us down. It's essential to restore order by understanding the nature of our thoughts and placing them where they belong, so they can support us rather than control us.

The mind is not aware of its own thoughts. Just as a knife cannot cut its own blade, thoughts cannot perceive themselves, but they do affect our experiences. We can truly become aware only by disentangling ourselves from identifying with our thoughts.

Remember this:

You are the one who thinks,
the one who acts,
the one who feels,
the one who observes.

The thinker is absorbed in thought,
the doer is busy doing,
the feeler is caught up in emotion.

Only the observer can hold space for all three.

No thought can contain you. You are not your perception; you hold the power to shape it. Your extraordinary experiences in the outside world occur within you, making them the closest thing to supernatural encounters you have every day. As you read these words, they are processed within you. Thoughts hold meanings, stories, ideas, and associations. Through your focused attention, they gain power. By deliberately directing your energy towards specific thoughts or ideas, you amplify their impact in shaping your actions and choices.

Ancient sages from various spiritual traditions understood the profound role of observers in shaping reality. In modern times, we have begun to see parallels in the micro-world of atoms and particles found in quantum mechanics. Scientists have generally agreed that the presence of an observer affects the reality being observed. In other words, observers are, in some sense, responsible for creating the reality that they see. Remarkably, any effort to observe a single particle alters its behavior.

Through your participatory awareness, your thoughts and perceptions become alive in you. And as you dwell in it, you create the world you live in, both individually and as part of a larger collective. Your triumphs, miseries, and complexities are all products of the mind, constantly shaping and reshaping your realities.

The good news is that your thoughts exist purely in the realm of ideas and imagination. They have no physical substance, so you can release them as quickly as you make them up. It is your choice whether you pay attention to them or not. As long as you desire them, they will appear before you; but once you let them go, in time, they will fade away from your focus.

You might ask, "What about all the problems we have in the world?" They persist irrespective of our awareness or lack thereof. The old and damaged buildings are still in the city, and the systems that have harmed nature and hurt people cannot be fixed overnight. The same goes for every single one of your personal problems.

Consider what Steve Jobs said when interviewed by the Santa Clara Valley Historical Association in 1994. When asked for his advice on how to best live life, he answered:

> When you grow up, you tend to get told that the world is the way it is, and your life is just to live your life inside the world —try not to bash into the walls too much, try to have a nice family life, have fun, save a little money. That's a very limited life.
>
> Life can be much broader once you discover one simple fact, and that is, everything around you that you call life was made up by people who were no smarter than you. And you can change it. You can influence it. You can build your own things that other people can use. The minute you understand

that you can poke life, and actually, something will pop out the other side—you can change it and mold it.

Maybe the most important thing is to shake off this erroneous notion that life is there and you're just going to live in it, versus embrace it, change it, improve it, make your mark upon it. I think that's very important. Once you learn it, you'll want to change life and make it better because it's kind of messed up in a lot of ways. Once you learn that, you'll never be the same again.

I invite you to digest this for a moment. The underlying fabric of the world you live in is not the brick and mortar but the mind. You have what Steve Jobs had—the power to change the world and make it a better place. It begins and ends in your mind. It is literally within you.

Consider this: the book you are reading and the chair you are sitting on would not have existed without existing as ideas first. Your own life, too, is formed by your mind by believing what you think is true to you. Through the act of thinking, we give birth to stories, ideas, inspirations, and beliefs that become the foundation of our understanding of the world.

A new choice doesn't begin when you make a decision. It starts from a shift in consciousness. As your awareness expands and evolves, your perspective changes.

Here lies the secret: the possibilities you are looking for are already present—*you* are the possibilities—for the one who thinks has a choice. What are you going to do with it?

REFLECTIONS AT YOUR OWN PACE

1. How might your beliefs and opinions influence your feelings and interactions with others?
2. What does it mean to disentangle ourselves from identifying with our thoughts?
3. Think about the concept of success and how it influences your life. What does success mean to you? How has society shaped your definition of success? Are there any mind-made constructs related to success that you adhere to or strive for?

THREE
THE FEAR-BASED OPERATING SYSTEM

We suffer from being fragments and being fragmented to the extent that we feel lonely, dependent, afraid, and in conflict with ourselves, and subject to desires that must be controlled. Much of human life is a succession of states of grasping, clutching, and yearning.

KABIR HELMINSKI

A story from an unknown author:
A gentleman strolled through the elephant camp, and a peculiar sight seized his attention. Not a single cage or chain confined the majestic elephants; instead, each colossal creature was tethered by a small piece of rope tied to its leg. The man couldn't believe his eyes! Despite their massive size and strength, the elephants made no attempt to break free.

Curious, he approached the trainer and asked why the elephants stood still and didn't try to escape.

The trainer chuckled and replied, "Well, when they were

little, we used the same tiny ropes to tie them up. At that age, the ropes were strong enough to hold them back. As they grew older, they simply never tried to break loose. They became conditioned to believe the rope could still hold them, so they never bothered to break free."

This is a story of humanity. From childhood, we've been taught that what we're doing now prepares us for what comes next. Elementary school sets the stage for high school. High school paves the way for university. University equips us for the long-haul race of our careers. As we enter the professional world, our gaze remains fixed on the horizon in the relentless pursuit of the "next thing." Even when we reach the pinnacle of success, we yearn for the distant shores of retirement, with its promised sense of liberation.

Our ambitions continue to evolve—from our first million dollars to the next and beyond. Growth, we believe, signifies progress. Yet, we often forget to reflect on what is behind our relentless pursuit of the next goal. Who we are and what we need never seem enough. The primal angst to get somewhere else and achieve something more remains unceasing.

In this free world, no one is held captive in a cage or bound by chains. But let's be honest—how many of us are being held by an invisible rope of fear? In our pursuit of more and better, how much time do we spend each day anticipating potential threats, no matter how trivial they might seem? Even those of us with substantial savings might grapple with the fear of job loss. We might think, "Am I safe if I lost my job? What happens if I can't get another job and end up penniless?"

In the same vein, even individuals with vast wealth and substantial investments can find themselves tossing and turning at night when the market experiences a downturn. They might ponder, "What if the market crashes and all my assets become worthless? How will I provide for my family and sustain my lifestyle?"

Our race, gender, age, or social and financial status are irrelevant; many of our thought patterns and behaviors are formed as responses to threats.

HOW OUR NERVOUS SYSTEM KEEPS US SAFE

Over millions of years, the human nervous system has evolved to aid our survival and adaptation. Its advanced survival system operates in three primary ways: self-preservation, self-maintenance, and reproduction. Among these, self-preservation is the most crucial, as the other facets cannot function properly without it. Our nervous system is built to support and regulate based on this hierarchy, constantly assessing our internal and external environment, calculating risks, and choosing the least threatening ways to stay alive.

When we feel safe, our parasympathetic nervous system activates, assisting in rest, digestion, and reproduction. But if a threat emerges, our sympathetic nervous system takes charge, initiating the fight-or-flight response by accelerating heart rate, releasing stress hormones, and directing blood flow to vital organs. This quick response helps us react swiftly to potential threats.

Even though we no longer need to defend ourselves against wild animals or warring tribes, our nervous system remains vigilant for potential modern-day threats. Our brains constantly scan our surroundings for potential harm, whether it's our clients, co-workers, spouses, neighbors, friends, news, social media, or even our thoughts.

When we sense a threat, our autonomous nervous system activates to determine the optimal strategy to ensure our safety. Past experiences are pivotal in molding our responses. If we've learned that being aggressive helped us overcome a threat in the past, we'll likely adopt the same approach in similar situations. If we've learned that avoiding conflict is the safest bet, we'll instinctively turn to that strategy. And if we've learned that disappearing is the best way to avoid danger, we'll quickly try to blend into the background.

But sometimes, when we feel trapped, we get stuck. Our minds can become overwhelmed with depression, helplessness, despair, shame, and dissociation, leaving us paralyzed and unable to act. This response is quite common in today's society.

SENSING SAFETY IN OUR INTERACTIONS AND THOUGHT PROCESSES

And here's more: our nervous system extends beyond its mechanical functions for biological survival; it also plays a vital role in helping us sense safety in social interactions.

The esteemed author of the groundbreaking Polyvagal Theory, Stephen Porges, has shed light on the intricate relationship between social engagement and our neurobiological survival mechanism. Through extensive research on the vagus nerve—a vital circuit responsible for regulating facial and head muscles while connecting the brain to crucial organs in your body—Porges has revealed a previously unknown fact: "We wear our hearts on our faces." This discovery uncovered the significance of facial expression patterns and vocal intonation in our ability to sense social safety cues. The neural connection from face to heart empowers us to discern calmness or agitation in others, serving as a crucial indicator for identifying safe interactions.

To illustrate this phenomenon, Porges shared an example involving two playful dogs. As they bark, nip at each other, and leap around, something remarkable happens—they always keep eye contact. Through their keen observation of facial expressions, they can quickly determine if the gestures are playful or edging towards aggression. Similarly, for us, this ability to detect subtle changes in facial expression and tone of voice is crucial to our survival and plays a fundamental role in our social interactions.

Expanding his studies to children's development, Porges made significant observations about safety and its deep ties to human connection. He says, "Safety is not just about the absence of threat but also the absence of connection." We become regulated and primed for engagement when we feel safe and secure. This state of safety fosters playfulness, creativity, and collaboration, opening doors for shared intimacy, authenticity, and joy. Children with a secure and loving relationship with their parents feel confident to explore and play, knowing they can always seek protection when needed. In contrast, children with attachment issues may be hesitant to venture far, uncertain about their safety, and fear they won't be accepted when they return.

Porges' Polyvagal Theory shows that our nervous system has wired the sense of safety as the foundation for forming human connections and relationships. In its absence, we instinctively construct walls and disconnect from others.

Now, let's delve into an example that demonstrates the connection between our cognitive processes and our physiological responses.

Picture yourself in a crowded room filled with strangers, the noise level rising to a deafening pitch. Your heart starts racing, and your palms become slick with sweat. Suddenly, your feet move without your conscious control, carrying you away from the chaos. Wouldn't that be a surreal and unsettling experience?

It would be because we need to have a sense of internal order and control to comprehend the unpredictable world. Life would be constantly overwhelming if we couldn't control or make sense of our movements and responses. To maintain your sense of self, any actions or behaviors must be perceived as under your control.

Returning to the scenario above, you need a compelling narrative to convince yourself to step away from the loud room full of strangers. Perhaps you told yourself that you decided to leave because the room was too crowded and too noisy; it made you anxious. Or maybe you decided you were bored and had no one to talk to. For whatever reason, you must be convinced that it was *you* who chose to leave the room, not your feet. Whatever reasons you have, they should make sense to you.

In this intricate interplay, nature uses our mental faculties to persuade us to take necessary actions, primarily for our survival and, subsequently, for our growth.

Human mental capacities find their roots in the architecture of the nervous system. While our biology predominantly relies on chemistry to process information, our mind processes it as a mental construct that can be cognitively perceived. Our advanced meaning-making capability makes a sense of safety intertwined in our thoughts, words, and narratives. Unlike other species, our survival mechanism isn't just wired for basic physical, relational, and emotional needs; it also encompasses our quest for meaning and purpose.

THE MOST POWERFUL DRIVE FOR SURVIVAL: FEAR

Our innate tendency to overestimate potential dangers has been crucial for our survival throughout history. Evolution has finely tuned our mind and body to detect and react to threats, enabling us to prepare for worst-case scenarios. For example, it's safer to mistake a dried, withered branch for a snake than to incorrectly perceive a venomous snake as a harmless branch, as the latter mistake can result in harm or death.

This instinctual fear response has been instrumental in shaping our actions across history. The fear of predatory animals drove early humans to develop tools, weapons, and communal living arrangements. During times of war and famine, fear motivated us to leave our homes in search of safety and new opportunities in foreign lands. In epidemics or pandemics, the fear of contracting a deadly illness has driven us to adopt measures for self-preservation and community protection. Fear has helped us discern what to avoid, fight, or overcome.

In survival mode, fear and control are intertwined. Our anticipation of threat, risk, and danger drives our need for control. The more we feel unsafe, the more we feel the need to have control over the situation. Stress, anxiety, burnout, and worry can arise when maintaining control requires significant effort.

A strong desire for control can cause us to lose touch with others and our own needs. We get wrapped up in the story we imagine might happen in an attempt to protect ourselves from an imagined, dreadful experience in the future. Instead of responding to the present moment, we react to the made-up story in our heads.

I'm sure you can find many examples in your own life where you're about to have a conversation with someone, but even before you meet them, your mind runs different scenarios about what you're going to say based on your past experiences with them. You might anticipate a difficult conversation before it happens, not realizing that when you eventually meet the person, you're engaging with them from the feeling created by the scenarios you ran in your head.

The need for control has created an imbalance of power and resources in our world. In his book, *The 9.9 Percent: The New Aristocracy That is Entrenching Inequality and Warping Our Culture*, Matthew Stewart, an Oxford-trained philosopher and former management consultant, explores the phenomenon of America's upper-middle class. They are the "haves," well-educated with great careers and high-paying jobs, and hyper-focused on getting their kids into excellent schools and extracurricular activities. They choose to reside in affluent neighborhoods and are willing to work harder and longer to pay for these opportunities and secure their children's future. However, the irony is that, despite being wealthy, they constantly compare themselves to someone richer. They consider themselves "struggling" because they must keep up with everyone else to avoid falling behind.

When asked in an interview about where this pressure comes from, Matthew Stewart says:

> I think the driving motivation is fear, and I think that fear is well-grounded. People intuit that in this meritocratic game, the odds are getting increasingly long of succeeding. They work very hard to stack the odds in their kids' favor, but they know as the odds get longer, they may not succeed. That's coupled with another one of the traits of this class, which is a lack of imagination. The source of the fear is also this inability to imagine a life that doesn't involve getting these high-status credentials and having a high-status occupation.

When the drive to succeed is based on our biologically ingrained fear of not having enough, there *never* will be enough. The race to have *more*, learn *more*, do *more*, and grow *more*, which can provide a fantastic feeling when we attain it, also results in discontentment. This discontentment persists not only when we fall short but even when we attain success, as we keep yearning for something more. Isn't our economy based on this too? We use scarcity tactics to make people buy more and work harder to keep the economy growing.

Even with all our advancements, it seems we're still very much living in survival mode. We hoard resources; driven by fear of the unknown and the imaginary scenarios we conjure in our minds. Humans have lived on Earth for more than 200,000 years, yet we're still wired to believe that what we seek is absent and must be pursued, claimed, and fought for. We're driven by primal fear and the belief that we'll never be enough if we're not constantly seeking, trying, and doing.

As Sadhguru, a spiritual teacher and global speaker, astutely observes:

> The most dominant aspect for most human beings today is security. Their lives are not about seeking joy and love; fundamentally, they seek security. Most of them are going after professional careers because that means security. They establish families mainly because that's another form of security; emotional security. Running after God is also security. Their whole life's energy is focused solely on their survival, nothing else. When you are too security-conscious, you naturally cannot live with abandon. In everything, you're held back. So, when you laugh, it doesn't go deep enough into you. When you love, it doesn't go deep enough into you. Even when you weep, it doesn't go deep enough into you. Because everything you do, you hold back. You always live with the fear that you may lose it.

Our modern lifestyle, wealth, and economic progress have not liberated us from this fear-based system. Instead, our progress perpetuates fear under a different name, revealing that despite our advancement, we remain enslaved. This insatiable hunger for security holds us captive, hindering our ability to enjoy life fully. But is it worth sacrificing our present contentment for the possibility of an unknown future? Perhaps it's time to reexamine our way of life and ask ourselves what we can do to break free from this cycle of fear and survival. It's time to thrive in a way that is good for our well-being and the planet.

REFLECTIONS AT YOUR OWN PACE

1. How often do you find yourself striving for the next achievement or milestone without reflecting on what you have accomplished and the person you have become?
2. Reflect on the role of fear in your drive for control. How does fear motivate your actions and decision-making processes? Are there areas of your life where fear prevents you from experiencing joy, love, and fulfillment?
3. Reflect on the true meaning of security for you. What does it mean to feel secure? How might you explore and develop a deeper understanding of your relationship with security?

FOUR
THE SURVIVAL MIND

> The future is by definition the unsayable and the uncontrollable, filled with paradoxes, mysteries, and confusions. It is an imperfect world at every level. Therefore, the future is always, somehow, scary. We attempt to build for ourselves many protections against this imperfection, even in the patterns of our mind. This unsayable future—preparing for it and also fearing it—determines much of our lives. Thus, we search for predictability, explanation, and order to give ourselves some sense of peace and control.
>
> RICHARD ROHR

In the past two centuries, the pace of progress has accelerated significantly. Our medical technology has improved, leading to an increase in life expectancy. Our food sources have been genetically modified for faster growth and better resilience in harsh environments, and commodity distribution networks have been greatly enhanced. The internet, mobile phones, and air travel have connected people like never before. More children now have access to education, including higher education. Our technology, knowledge, and information are no longer exclusive—everything we need to know is available at our fingertips within seconds. The next advancement, artificial intelligence, will soon be able to perform most of the doing and thinking for us.

Technology and innovations have made things easier, faster, and more effective in virtually every aspect of our lives. But despite these achievements, why does the fear deep within our psyche remain unsolved?

If we were to collect our thoughts and categorize them according to their nature, we'd find an endless row of fearful thoughts of all shapes and sizes. Fear of public opinion—what will my colleagues think? Fear of rejection—what if people don't like me? Fear of failure—what if I don't succeed in my marriage, business, or other endeavors? Fear of the unknown—what if I don't know what to do? Fear of living, fear of dying, fear of making mistakes, fear of abandonment, fear of pain, fear of suffering ...

Yet, despite our efforts to overcome our fears, we seem to be left with fear itself, ready to let it overshadow the next thing we pay attention to. We fear what we worry might happen—that our spouse might leave us, that we might lose our job, that our investments might fail, and that our children might disappoint us. This anticipatory thinking, driven by fear, prevents us from focusing on what *is* and fixates our attention on what isn't. No wonder we struggle to find contentment and happiness, for these can only be found in the present moment, in what truly *is*, not what *isn't*. So why do we continue to doubt and inflict negativity upon ourselves? It makes absolutely no sense, logically or otherwise.

As a child growing up in Indonesia, I remember an Indonesian proverb, "Prepare your umbrella before it rains." It taught me the importance of being proactive and prepared for whatever challenges may come our way. After all, it's always better to be safe than sorry. As our world increasingly relies on technology and infrastructure, we have developed a strong desire for predictability. Like having a parachute before we jump, we want to know what lies ahead before we take any action and mitigate potential risks before they arise.

Isn't it funny that, while much of our mental energy is directed toward achieving our goals, if you take a closer look, you'll realize that what truly drives us is an effort to avoid what we *do not want to happen*?

So long as we cling to this survival strategy, we will not be free from psychological fear. For what we don't know, we can't control.

Here is a great example. It's from a post I found in one of the writer's Facebook groups that I belong to:

> For years, I've been wanting to write, I am obsessed with analyzing stories, poetry, films, songs, etc., and I feel I have learnt enough to be able to write my own. Now I'm concerned, because getting published, and getting it out there, I'm constantly told is beyond difficult, and what were meant to be warnings from well-meaning writers, has turned into a very serious doubt that writing is just an absolute waste of time. I've been told numerous times that it is nearly impossible to get published, extremely difficult to even get a publisher to read what you've written, and that earning any

money from what you've written would practically be pocket money. Could someone please explain why they believe I'm wrong? Why do you write, despite the fact that what you're writing is almost going to be in vain?

From what I comprehend, it seems this person has not done much writing, or maybe not at all. But see how many reasons and future scenarios they have created in their mind even before they start? Can you imagine how hard it must be to write with all those doubts and fears? That's a whole lot of resistance and agony right there!

Fear is a state of avoidance, a resistance to action. It compels us to flee and avoid the experience of dealing with unpleasant emotions. In response, our minds skim the surface, falling into a trance of busyness, preventing us from staying present and doing the necessary work. Our mental resources and imagination capacity are consumed by anticipating what might happen. As a result, we come to believe that what we do not know or understand has power over us. Therefore, it must be controlled and overcome.

When fear drives us, it limits our perspective and narrows our options. For example, people often stay in jobs they dislike because they worry that they won't be able to afford their expenses if they quit. Fear can stop us from exploring other possibilities that could lead to a more fulfilling life.

Without realizing it, every day, we engage in what I call "survival mind"—a prolonged state of hyper vigilance where we rely heavily on our Head Space to preconceive possible scenarios, predict outcomes, and devise solutions in anticipation of future events. This pattern serves as a coping mechanism that aims to give us a sense of control and security.

However, the constant cycle of anticipation and prediction inhibits our ability to fully engage and embrace the present moment.

In this state, fear not only captures our attention, logic, and imagination, but it also impacts our ability to care and love. When operating from our survival mind, love and care can morph into an obsession to control and protect rather than being present for those we love.

Imagine a parent who loves their child dearly and wants nothing but the best for them. However, when that love is crippled with fear, it can lead to overprotectiveness and excessive control. While some level of concern is natural, constantly worrying about their child's safety, well-being, or future can cause a parent to become overly restrictive and micromanage every aspect of their child's life. This behavior may seem like an act of love, but in reality, it often stems from the need for control rather than genuine care for the child's growth and development. Ultimately, such constant monitoring not only harms the child's independence but also makes them unable to learn from their mistakes—which are essential parts of growing up and developing resilience.

When we're absorbed in the anticipatory habits of our survival mind, we often overlook those aspects of our lives that work well, feel effortless, and bring us joy. In a vigilant state where safety and security are top priorities, we naturally focus on problems and deficiencies. Many unpleasant feelings —such as worry, frustration, anxiety, disappointment, anger, stress, overwhelm, and doubt—stem from the underlying fears that permeate our thoughts. These feelings do not derive from actual events but rather from our interpretations and expectations of what should or shouldn't happen and the significance we attach to them. When all we can see is what's lacking, it becomes challenging to cultivate gratitude and contentment. Likewise, it can be hard to remain open and relaxed when we don't feel safe.

Someone I know shared his experience taking his seven-year-old son to a water park. They started with the smaller rides and gradually moved toward the bigger ones. That's when they saw it: the tallest water slide his son was eligible to ride.

"Can we go on that one, Dad?" the son asked.

"Of course," the dad replied, and they walked up the stairs to the top of the slide. But as soon as they reached the top, the boy froze. He looked down and felt scared.

"I don't think I can do it," he told his dad.

"That's okay," his dad said. "You can try again later when you feel more comfortable."

The boy tried a few more times by himself, but he felt too scared to go down the slide after reaching the top, so he walked down the stairs instead.

On the fifth attempt, the boy's father stood at the bottom of the water slide, expecting his son to retreat down the stairs once again. But as he looked up, he saw his son zooming down the slide with a wide grin on his face. The boy crashed into the water and swam over to the pool's edge. His face was beaming with joy.

Filled with pride and curiosity, the father asked, "What made you conquer your fear and go down the slide?"

The boy answered, "Well, I was up there, feeling scared and unsure, but then I slipped, and suddenly I was sliding down!"

He looked at his dad with excitement and continued, "I want to do it again, Dad!"

This lighthearted story brought to mind a perspective shared by Jiddu Krishnamurti, a prolific philosopher and teacher. He was once asked by an interviewer about the fear of death. He replied, "Thought is the origin of fear. If death were to happen right away, there would be no fear. But if it were to happen in ten days' time, then thoughts would begin to think about it."

Like the boy in the story, we spend much of our time and energy in anticipation. Fear doesn't live in the present; it arises when your mind is fixated on what 'might' happen. No matter how much you overthink a situation, it often only takes you a split second to decide and act. When you actually do something you are afraid of, you simply do it without the long and painful thought process. Doubting ourselves and worrying does not make anything better, but that is what we tend to do.

THE NATURE OF THE SURVIVAL MIND

Michael Graziano, a distinguished neuroscientist, has devoted his research to the fascinating question of how our brain processes attention and awareness. He has put forward a groundbreaking theory known as the Attention Schema Theory (AST). This theory explains how our brain creates a simplified model to monitor and control our attention, much like it forms an internal map of our body to regulate our movements. According to Graziano, consciousness arises as a solution to the fundamental problem faced by all nervous systems: the need to process an overwhelming amount of information. In essence, AST suggests that our attention awareness is a product of the brain's necessity to manage and make sense of the continuous influx of sensory data and internal processes it encounters.

Consider what it would be like to be conscious of every single detail of the world around us. Imagine being acutely aware of Earth's electromagnetic currents; every single internal organ in our body; or the growth of a tree, leaf, or fruit. Think of how it would feel to perceive every single thought other people have when we talk to them. It would be impossible to process all this information and still function normally.

Cognitive scientist Donald Hoffman has a brilliant metaphor to illustrate how natural selection has shaped us to take in only the most essential information. When you see a folder icon on your desktop, it doesn't mean that the folder where you store your text files is located there or that the folder is blue. The screen and the icon are just an interface to make it easier for you to access the file quickly. Imagine navigating through the diodes, resistors, the electric current, and the megabytes of data to locate and retrieve the file you need. It would be a nightmare! Our brain also works like a desktop interface to present us with a simplified model of the world around us, allowing us to perceive only what is necessary for survival.

Selective attention allows us to efficiently process information, but it also means that we may overlook important details that are not immediately relevant to our survival or goals. Similarly, we only see fragments of the whole picture when we think and analyze. When this way of perceiving becomes our default operating system, it's easy to forget that life encompasses more than what meets the eye.

Language perfectly demonstrates our selective nature. Imagine introducing yourself to a stranger; just because they know your name doesn't mean they know everything about you. You cannot be contained by words. Even in lengthy conversations, elaborating on your experiences, thoughts, and emotions only scratches the surface of your full complexity. Strangers can only glimpse a fraction of who you are.

In the same vein, when you name or label an object with a word, you confine its existence to your definition. For example, when you say something is "black," you imply it is not white or any other color. When you label an object as a "tree," you limit it to just that and nothing else.

Now, you may be asking: What is the issue with labeling?

The problem is that once we construct an understanding of something in our minds, it becomes harder to see the object beyond the label and its complex reality. We disconnect from it. For example, this phenomenon is evident in how we stereotype people based on their race, making it challenging to perceive them as fellow human beings with the same needs, challenges, and dreams as ourselves.

In our evolutionary history, prioritizing differences over similarities was paramount to our survival. This preference proved crucial when the ability to swiftly discern between predators and non-predators meant the difference between life and death. Consequently, our brains have evolved to prioritize differences over commonalities, with optimal learning arising from identifying and comparing distinctions among objects.

However, labeling and comparing reveal the constraints of

our intellectual and analytical prowess. These faculties operate based on accumulated knowledge and past experiences. Comprehension requires an existing understanding, and comparisons require a reference point rooted in prior knowledge. Unknowingly, we develop a deeply entrenched habit of pre-determining *what is* or *what will be* based on our past experiences.

Everything you have and do today is a continuation of your mind from yesterday and the days before. As you navigate through life, your brain retrieves memories from the past and rearranges them to make sense of the present. You don't have to relearn how to talk or read every day because your mind is full of memories that let you pick up where you left off. Imagine waking up and not remembering who your loved ones are or how to operate your coffee maker. Can you picture the challenge?

The reliance on past references becomes evident in our interactions and relationships. Suppose you find yourself in a challenging conversation with a client. Drawing from your past experiences, you might assume the situation will take a negative turn. This assumption prompts you to strategize and adjust the situation based on previously learned conflict resolution behaviors. Your expectations and anticipatory mental efforts to control the situation prevent you from being receptive and open to the situation at hand, which may demand a different response. The same applies to any relationship, including those with family, your partner, or friends.

This is when learning often becomes stagnant: When logic and reasoning merely serve to reinforce your narrative and affirm existing beliefs. In such a mindset, every event, idea, and person is filtered through the lens of what you already know, agree with, or find familiar. Anything that doesn't fit into these categories is perceived as a potential threat or labeled as wrong. (After all, isn't that what judgment is?) Even the fear of losing one's identity stems from the apprehension of stepping into the unknown and leaving behind familiar comforts.

CANNOT TOLERATE THE UNKNOWN

Our minds clearly perform at their best in familiar territory, which is why proven methodologies are so effective.

For instance, in the dynamic area of marketing, seasoned professionals often rely on well-established strategies with a track record of success, such as target audience segmentation and proven content marketing techniques to reel in customers with a magnetic pull.

Our analytical abilities hold great value as they help us to recognize recurring patterns and employ established strategies to achieve desired outcomes. We repeat familiar things we already know throughout our lives, such as talking, walking, driving a car, and performing tasks at work. In fact, in our professional occupations, we learn to repeat what we do well and are financially rewarded for doing so.

Yet, the very proficiency that serves us well throughout most of our lives can lose its effectiveness in unfamiliar territory. Relying solely on accumulated knowledge to navigate the future can prove misleading. We might be tempted to believe that we have everything under control, but uncertainty remains an inherent aspect of our existence. There is always a gap between what we know and the unknown. Fear, a potent motivator in both actions and inactions, often compels us to view the unknown as a problem that needs a solution.

Here lies the agony of modern humans!

We yearn to unleash our freedom and potential, yet we fiercely grasp onto our craving for control. The irony is that we cannot achieve our freedom and potential without embracing uncertainty.

The good news? The unknown is fertile ground for possibility.

As Fr. Richard Rohr puts it:

> If you surrender to the fear of uncertainty, life can become a set of insurance policies. Your short time on this earth becomes small and self-protective, a kind of circling of the wagons around what you can be sure of and what you think you can control—even God. It provides you with the illusion that you are in the driver's seat, navigating on safe, small roads, and usually in a single, predetermined direction that can take you only where you have already been.

We must be willing to embrace a different approach when we find ourselves at the juncture where the known ends and the unknown begins. In this space, we must let go of our natural tendency to dissect, solve, and hastily judge circumstances, recognizing that trying to control what we don't yet fully comprehend is fruitless.

Putting aside the impulse to solve problems and, instead, making room for something new is not a behavior that the survival mind readily adopts. On the contrary, the survival mind grapples with gaps and ambiguity. It craves resolution and finality, and it wants them promptly. It becomes consumed with evaluating, quantifying, interpreting, justifying, and creating meaning—all in the relentless pursuit of finding the right answer and making sense of everything.

Regrettably, the Head Space that gives rise to the survival mind can only use past experiences as a reference to predict the future, thus preventing it from achieving full certainty about what lies ahead. In fact, the mind can only speculate and entertain thoughts of certainty. It is incapable of experiencing it, for true certainty exists in a felt-sense experience, not just a mere thought. When confronted with situations that do not make sense, the Head Space can only bridge the gap by rearranging what's familiar and creating a modified version of the same narrative. It cannot accept what it can't comprehend.

When fear grips you, your mind seeks refuge from the terrifying unknown, growing restless in its quest for answers. It tirelessly analyzes the situation from every conceivable angle, often without us even realizing it. If we push it too far, we become trapped in a cycle of repetitive thoughts, much like a hamster running endlessly on a wheel. This state is often expressed as feeling "stuck," "paralyzed," "frustrated," or "sleep-deprived" due to incessant overthinking.

For instance, consider one of my coaching clients, who sought my guidance during her recent divorce. Facing the abrupt change, she became consumed by questions of "why" and constantly justified her story. Trapped in a cycle of "would've," "should've," and "could've" thinking, she desperately tried to make sense of her divorce. The weight of the situation led her to internalize the label of "failure." The hypervigilant and anticipatory nature of her survival mind painted her a bleak future filled with worry and uncertainty.

This mental turmoil had a significant effect on her, making it hard for her to stay focused at work and get restful sleep.

Throughout our coaching journey, I created a safe and nurturing space for her to explore her grief, honor her feelings, and find solace. Our work involved understanding not only her challenges and fears from a logical perspective but also delving into her Heart Space.

By creating a safe space for her emotions and self-discovery, she began seeing new possibilities and opening to them. Her self-doubt and fear lessened as she showed self-compassion and gained a deeper understanding of her needs and desires. Over time, her view of the future changed from being defined by the past to being shaped by her newfound self-awareness and resilience. During our brief time together, I witnessed her transformation. She regained her confidence and realized that her divorce didn't define her worth or future. She even considered dating again, expanding her horizons and embracing fresh opportunities.

The survival mind is not interested in fostering clear thinking or gaining new insights from your circumstances. It will always move toward its own logic, isolating you from seeing the whole picture.

It's important to recognize that often, we don't respond to actual events but rather to the interpretations we tell ourselves about those events. Once these perceptions are locked in our minds, we close ourselves to any possibilities that don't fit our preconceived notions. This self-imposed limitation prevents us from fully experiencing the power of transformation that emerges when we make room for new and unexpected possibilities.

Like my coaching client, we must transition from the

Head Space to the Heart Space, releasing the grip of our survival mind's need for control. This shift enables us to gain valuable insights into life's obstacles. The Heart Space empowers us to envision a future free from the constraints of our past.

THE SEPARATED SELF AND THE SURVIVAL MIND

Deep down, many of us feel disconnected from who we really are. It's as if we are detached from our deepest thoughts, desires, and wisdom, leaving us feeling lost and yearning for a sense of wholeness. Our inner orphans carry these feelings and struggle to find their place in the world.

In response to this disconnection, we build walls of intellectual armor, relying on reason and control to face the world. We create a long list of self-imposed rules and guidelines to maintain a sense of certainty and shield ourselves from uncomfortable emotions. We become consumed by the compulsion to quantify and predict, constantly keeping ourselves busy to ward off fear and doubt. Without realizing it, we are not living our lives; we are trapped in the pattern of survival, missing out on the opportunity to enjoy life as it naturally unfolds.

The belief that everything in life must be earned, that success demands hard work and competition, and that time is a limited resource reflects a fundamental survival stance that has shaped our modern understanding of the world. Even positive mindsets are often rooted in these survival frameworks.

At the core of our survival consciousness lies a constant

state of angst and inadequacy that permeates every aspect of our lives. Society harnesses this condition to motivate ambitious individuals, convincing them they lack what they desire and must work hard to attain it. Many of us use fear as a driving force to excel, meet deadlines, and achieve audacious goals. However, this perpetual sense of separation and scarcity leaves us feeling incomplete. We are constantly longing for something better and bigger, often forgetting that joy, peace, ease, and flow are our natural state of being.

In our childhood, we effortlessly experienced moments of pure being without needing self-development courses or expertise in meditation and mindfulness. Yet, as we grew, we made simplicity complex, mistakenly believing that more control and effort would lead to greater results.

When we become consumed by a rigid, dualistic way of thinking, we risk losing touch with the beating, passionate center of our being—one that is always there and never leaves! We become strangers to ourselves, cut off from the boundless joy and wonder that comes from embracing the full spectrum of our human experience.

What we truly need is a shift in consciousness, and it's only through expanding our awareness and being open to the unknown that we can embrace life's beautiful paradoxes:

> When you let go of control,
> you have more control.

> When you allow total vulnerability,
> you gain freedom.

> When you accept,

you find peace.

When you trust,
you gain clarity.

When you let go of resistance,
you experience ease and flow.

When you remove judgment,
you welcome authenticity.

When you let go of the obsession to be productive and have a meaningful life, you find pleasure in ordinary things.

As you shift your awareness from your Head Space to the Heart Space, a profound transformation happens. You begin to see the intricate and interconnected web that binds everything together. This shift widens your perspective, enabling you to see beyond the surface. You develop a greater sense of ease in living with the mysteries of life. As you gain a deeper understanding that life will unfold as it should, worries and fears dissipate.

When you come to a place where you truly see and accept all that you are, the constant need to seek *more* falls away. It is replaced with a sense of inner peace and contentment that remains unshaken by external circumstances.

The beloved Buddhist monk Thich Nhat Hanh beautifully depicts this concept with a metaphor:

> If you pour a handful of salt into a cup of water, the water becomes undrinkable. But if you pour the salt into a river, people can continue to draw the water to cook, wash, and

drink. The river is immense, and it has the capacity to receive, embrace, and transform.

When we reside in our Head Space, isolated and detached from life's flow, we resemble water in a cup. Our capacity to embrace fear and navigate the patterns of survival remains limited, closed, and narrow, much like the confines of our finite minds. In contrast, our Heart Space is like a river, entwined with the tapestry of life. Thus, we possess the capacity to hold paradoxes, contradictions, and a myriad of feelings. Our immense connection with the boundless river of life empowers us to transmute fear into love, resistance into acceptance, control into letting go, stagnation into flow, and trauma into healing. We become fluid, adaptable, and open to the full spectrum of experiences that life offers.

Undoubtedly, our reliance on the cup of our mind is too limiting.

As Fr. Richard Rohr wrote in *Falling Forward*:

Yes, the mind is necessary, but it can't do everything.

Yes, the mind is receptive, but reason is not our only antenna. We also need our bodies, our emotions, our hearts, our nose, our ears, our eyes, our taste, and our souls.

Yes, the mind can achieve great things, but through overcontrol, it can also limit what we can know.

Yes, the mind can think great thoughts, and also bad and limiting ones.

Yes, the mind can tell left from right, but it cannot perceive invisible things such as love, eternity, fear, wholeness, mystery, or the Divine.

Yes, the mind can discern consistency, logic, and fairness, but it seldom puts these into practice.

Yes, the mind and reason are necessary, but they must learn to distinguish between what lies beyond its reach: the prerational and the transrational.

Yes, the mind is brilliant, but the more we observe it, the more we see it is also obsessive and repetitive.

Yes, the mind seeks the truth, but it can also create lies.

Yes, the mind can connect us with others, but it can also keep us apart.

Yes, the mind is very useful, but when it does not recognize its own finite viewpoint, it is also useless.

Yes, the mind can serve the world, but in fact it largely serves itself.

Yes, the mind can make necessary distinctions, but it also divides in thought what is undivided in nature and in the concrete.

Yes, the mind is needed, but we also need other ways of knowing or we will not know well, fully, or freely.

Are you ready to live from your Heart Space?

REFLECTIONS AT YOUR OWN PACE

1. How often do you find yourself consumed by fearful thoughts about the future? Are these fears based on actual threats, or are they driven by anticipation and a need for control?
2. Reflect on a recent situation where you allowed fear to limit your perspective and narrow your options. What possibilities did you miss out on due to your survival mind?
3. How does the need for control and predictability affect your ability to engage with the present moment? Do you struggle to find contentment and happiness because your focus is constantly on what's lacking or what might go wrong?

SUMMARY: QUALITIES OF THE HEAD SPACE

Activate through thinking, you know you are operating from the Head Space when you observe the presence of these traits:

- **Conceptual:** understands reality through abstract ideas; operates in a state of detachment ("being apart") as opposed to a state of connection ("being with").
- **Analytical:** constantly breaks down information into smaller components for intellectual comprehension; prioritizes "knowing about" over "knowing through."
- **Narrow Focus:** directs attention to a specific aspect while filtering out broader complexities.
- **Delimitative:** has the tendency to confine exploration to specific details or a particular difference.
- **Reductive:** simplifies and breaks down information to reduce complexity.

- **Anticipatory:** seeks to predict and control outcomes by generating possible scenarios.
- **Intolerant of the Unknown:** unable to accept what it can't comprehend; prefers to engage in overthinking rather than accepting that it doesn't know.
- **Comparison-Based:** categorizes and evaluates experiences by comparing them to similar or contrasting situations, ideas, or standards.
- **Rigid:** over-dependent on established paradigms and existing knowledge to grasp new information; manifests as an unwillingness to accept or integrate new information if it contradicts pre-existing beliefs or knowledge.
- **Fragmented:** splits and categorizes information, fragmenting the perception of reality into discrete parts.
- **Needs Proof:** constantly seeks supporting evidence to validate ideas and beliefs, prioritizing factual backing.
- **Thrives in Doubt:** activated when facing information gaps; engages in persistent questioning and explores endless potential narratives to convince itself.
- **Strives for Control:** attains a sense of control through logical reasoning. Inherently driven to seek closure and definitive resolutions.

These traits are not good or bad; they function as tools that can be valuable in specific situations. They enhance our abilities in completing tasks, such as strategic planning, analysis, project management, legal compliance, and goal-oriented pursuits. However, they may also limit our capacity to think in new ways and adapt to uncertainty.

THE SURVIVAL MIND

When fear dominates, survival mechanisms can quickly take over your Head Space. Your mind becomes hyper-vigilant in this mode, fixating on what's "missing." This constant state of apprehension engages your cognitive capacity in a loop of anticipating negative outcomes and formulating solutions in preparation for those potential results—all are hypothetical in nature. This coping mechanism aims to provide a sense of control and security in the face of uncertainty. Paradoxically, it ends up being the force that sustains fear.

Now you know, there is nothing "wrong" with you when you are overwhelmed by fear or anxiety. It's simply a common response that arises when your cognitive abilities go into overdrive. Fear is your mind's attempt to keep you out of its perceived danger. Understanding the intricacies of your thought processes will lead to greater self-awareness and a deeper understanding of yourself.

In the next section, we'll explore the notion of the Heart Space and its power to guide us toward a life of ease, grace, and freedom.

SECTION TWO: THE HEART SPACE

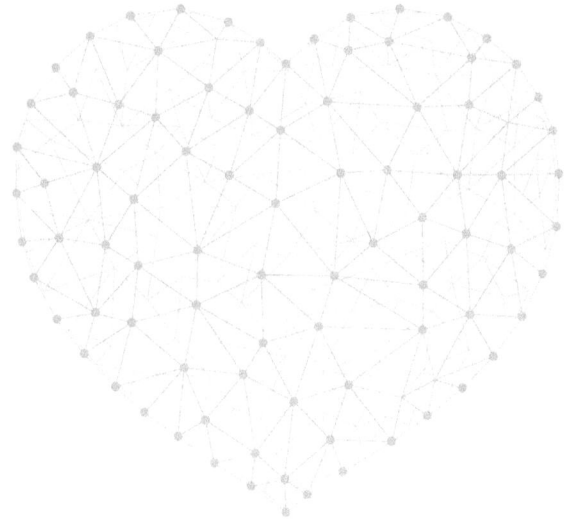

The Chinese character Xin

The heart as a center of the mind is not a new concept. The ancient Chinese believed the heart was the center of human cognition. The Chinese character Xin (心) is used for both "mind" and "heart." This character resembles a heart and literally refers to the physical heart, but it is also used to represent the mind, heart, center, and core. That is why it is often translated as "heart-mind."

In Japanese, there's no specific character for "mind." The word *Kokoro* when written the same as Chinese kanji 心, also means heart. When it refers to the mind, it unites the notions of heart, mind, and spirit.

In the rich tapestry of ancient mystic wisdom, spanning from the East to the West, encompassing the enigmatic realms of Sufism, Buddhism, Hinduism, and Christianity to the contemplative insights of the desert fathers, a common thread emerges: the heart, not the brain, is the gateway to higher consciousness.

Modern science has revealed that the heart is more than a cardiac pump. It possesses its own neural network—an intricate "little brain" containing around 40,000 neurons known as sensory neurites. Research conducted by the HeartMath Institute has illuminated the remarkable neural circuitry of this heart-brain, allowing it to function independently of the cranial brain. It can learn, remember, make functional decisions, and experience feelings and sensations. The heart sends more signals to the brain than the brain to the heart. It uses four different pathways: neurologically, through afferent and efferent impulses of the vagus nerve; biochemically, via hormones and neurotransmitters; biophysically, through pulse waves; and energetically, through electromagnetic fields.

The heart's magnetic field is the strongest rhythmic field produced by the human body. It not only envelops every cell of the body but also extends out into the space around us in all directions. It can be detected by other individuals and can produce measurable effects in a person five feet away.

When you direct your awareness to your heart center, you can experience a noticeable change. You'll feel it in your body, state of mind, and energy levels as a greater sense of groundedness. Cynthia Bourgeault, an author and a scholar of contemplative tradition, has described the somatic experience when we shift our center of gravity to the heart: "It's a mindful, fierce, attentiveness in your body, grounded in your feet, deeply in contact with our motherly Earth, centered lower than your head, in the region of your heart and your torso . . . as a whole alert presence." She continues, "In this configuration, not only are you truly present, it communicates. It has a force; it beams out and gives and receives it as its own kind of sonar . . . When the mind comes into the heart, a different kind of knowingness happens."

The heart generates an expansive, holistic, encompassing way of seeing. It allows us to be more alive, awake, and connected so that we can respond from a higher level of consciousness rather than from the ingrained habits and old patterns of the Head Space.

Prepare yourself to see the world with a renewed sense of openness, curiosity, and connection in the chapters ahead.

FIVE
SEEING THROUGH THE HEART

And now here is my secret, a very simple secret: It is only with the heart that one can see rightly; what is essential is invisible to the eye.

ANTOINE DE SAINT-EXUPÉRY

●

What do you see above?

Most likely, your answer is a "black dot" or a "circle." But there is something else. Can you guess?

Isn't it interesting that we often overlook the very thing that enables us to perceive the circle? That empty space is much larger than the circle, yet it goes unnoticed by our awareness.

Can you identify another invisible element that enables you to see the dot?

The answer is light. The light that fills the room you're sitting in is invisible, yet the objects around you become visible through its presence. Similarly, space is invisible to your physical eyes. You become aware of space and distance only through the objects you see around you. You know how big a room is by measuring the walls that enclose the room. In the same vein, only when we gaze upon the countless stars, we catch a glimpse of the infinite depths of outer space.

You can read the words on this page because of the white space. It allows you to see the shape of the letters.

The air you breathe, which you can't live without, is invisible to your eyes.

Can you see love? No, you can't. You can only feel it.

The way you see defines what you see. When your way of seeing is rushed, merely skimming the surface, the screen in your mind projects the old, stale pictures and feelings retrieved from your memory. Nothing new arises.

When you are caught up in the survival mind, all you see is the black dot—what you lack, what's missing, and what's wrong. The abundant possibilities and opportunities become invisible. It clouds your hope, muddies your trust, and bends your focus.

We miss much more when we believe the only way to see is through the eyes and the only way to understand is through our intellect.

Yes, our eyes and minds are useful. They allow us to navigate the physical world with precision. But they represent just one way of seeing and knowing. The mind, in particular, tends to store snapshots from the past, akin to images in a photograph, which remain unaltered. These outdated mental references are then compared with our present circumstances.

I invite you to take a minute and look away from this book. Observe what's right in front of you.

Your eyes recognize everyday objects in no time:

a chair,
a wall,
a window,
books on the shelf,
and the ceiling above.

Have you ever noticed how you inadvertently overlook the finer details as you name these items?

The texture of the chair, the way sunlight penetrates the window, and the shape and pattern of the curtain.

Why? It's because the moment your eyes fixate on an object, your mind recalls an image of that same object from yesterday.

When you rely on what you know, it is easy to lose sight of the details. Thus, our capacity to capture details and newness in our moment-by-moment experience diminishes.

It's fascinating how readily we assume that "seeing" something equates to truly "knowing" it. This inclination leads us to assume that merely knowing something is the same as experiencing it. However, true encounters only occur when we take the time to engage our senses and connect with what is in front of us. Take, for example, a scrumptious piece of chocolate cake; it's only when you sink your teeth into it, allowing your taste buds to savor its luscious flavors, that you experience its fullness. Too often, people presume they "know" the taste of chocolate cake without even touching or eating it simply because they've eaten similar cakes before. This subtle deception created by the brain—mainly for survival and efficiency—raises a fundamental question:

> *How much of what we think we encounter in the present is actually a projection of the past?*

Once, I sat by a creek in a meditative state, observing a small area where water flowed between two rocks. The water's current was exceptionally vivid in that spot, and I found myself mesmerized by its fluid form.

As my mind quieted, I had an epiphany: though the water flowing against the rock appeared unchanging, it was, in fact, an ever-changing stream. My eyes saw stillness, but beneath the calm surface, an unceasing current flowed.

The Irish singer-songwriter Van Morrison appears to grasp the deception. In his song, he expresses his yearning, "If my heart could do my thinking, and my head begin to feel, I would look upon the world anew, and know what's truly real."

It's easy to overlook things we believe we've encountered before. But how can we cultivate a deeper sensibility, letting our hearts guide our perception to see the world anew?

EXPERIENCING A TRUE ENCOUNTER

Poet and priest John O'Donohue writes in *Divine Beauty: The Invisible Embrace*, "Seeing is not merely a physical act." He continues, "There are many things near us that we never notice simply because of the way we see. The way we look at things has a huge influence on what becomes visible for us."

In *Naked Now*, Fr. Richard Rohr uses "encounter" as another word for "presence." He describes the encounter as "a different way of knowing and touching the moment. It is much more vulnerable and leaves us without a sense of control." You cannot start seeing or understanding anything in an encounter if you start with "No." He says, "You have to start with 'Yes' of basic acceptance . . . , which means not too quickly labeling, analyzing, or categorizing things, in or out, good or bad. You have to leave the field open."

The open field is an unknown territory for our dualistic and controlling mind. Yet, only when we find ourselves in this open space can we discover new possibilities and a whole new perspective.

Rather than leaving this idea as a mental concept, I invite you to experience a true encounter in a simple experiment. In the following pages, you'll find easy-to-follow instructions. As you read them, imagine yourself following the instructions. Later, after reading this book, you can try it on your own.

Are you ready?

Standing where you are, begin by closing your eyes.

Take a deep breath to center yourself.

Then, slowly raise one foot off the ground
and start walking with your eyes closed.

As you can't rely on your eyesight and need to feel
your way, you begin to slow down.

Your body starts to tap into a different way of navigating space.

Your ability to sense movement, position,
and space heightens.

You listen, not just with your ears,
but also, with your skin.

You become more receptive
to your surrounding sounds.

You pace your breath naturally.

From identifying space through objects,
you shift your focus to spatial awareness.

You become more aware of not just the space in front of you, but also to the left, right, above, below, and behind.

Your relationship with the three-dimensional space changes.

You access your memory of the space in a different way, not through thinking, but through feeling and sensing the room.

There is gentleness in your movement.

Because you don't want to fall or bump into something hard, you soften your touch.

As you broaden your senses,
you become more aware of your center and balance.

The relationship between you and everything around you changes, because the way you navigate space changes.

Since you can't see, you let go of what you know and rely more on what is here, now.

This quality of softness, gentleness, and open awareness you carry in your body penetrates your mind and calms your worry of falling or stumbling.

The feedback you receive from hearing and sensing in real-time, both inward and outward, gives you vast awareness of space and the relationship between you and the external world.

Did you notice something different happening? This kind of seeing might leave you feeling vulnerable and perhaps make you lose your sense of control. But you didn't rush to impose what you knew during the experiment. You gave yourself time to observe, sense, and feel with your whole being. You continuously felt your way through and sensed your position in relation to the space around you. You were alert but in a relaxed way. You paused deliberately, allowing your sensory experience to guide your movements. Your mind was not fixated on discerning the right or wrong way to move, nor did you try to guess where you would be ten steps ahead. You were not even thinking; you went with the flow. The boundary between you and the outer world softened. You became one with your movement, and your movement was one with space. You perceived this profound connectedness from the depth of your experience. You didn't just have an idea or a thought about something—you encountered it. You touched it as it touched you. In that moment, what to do became obvious. This gathered presence creates a resonance between your inner and outer worlds. Through the resonance, a different kind of knowing emerges.

This is what it feels like when you live from the Heart Space.

While your eyes are limited to surface appearances, your heart can attune to frequency vibrations, feelings, and sensations. It goes beyond the definite and defined. In this state, you can experience the open field many enlightened spiritual teachers have pointed out.

Rumi depicts the open field as a "garden." He writes, "Somewhere beyond right and wrong, there is a garden. I will meet you there."

Victor Frankl describes it as "space." He says, "Between stimulus and response, there is a space. In that space is our power to choose our response. In our response lies our growth and our freedom."

This garden or space always exists within the realm of the heart. It stays open, invites exploration, and remains receptive. Through the heart, you are guided by a different kind of precision—a precision that doesn't arise from erecting barriers, categorizing objects as good versus bad, or rigidly defining right and wrong. Instead, it stems from the act of unification, bringing everything into harmony. It allows you to peer into the essence of an object rather than merely perceiving its superficial features, to see *through* and *into* it rather than just *at* it. Through the essence, you apprehend the whole. By comprehending the whole, you begin to realize that nothing is apart.

While writing this chapter, my dad passed away. Although my family knew it was coming, confronting the reality that I couldn't see him again, not even through a video call from his home in Jakarta, was difficult. With his passing, I felt as though a piece of my heart had gone missing. When my sister shared the news, I felt deeply sad, as if a giant wave had engulfed me. For days, I mourned in solitude in Toronto. I attended the ceremonies remotely, talking daily with my sisters and mother. I watched old friends and relatives bid farewell to my dad via my sister's phone. He had wished to be cremated, and one of the final videos my sister sent me captured the aftermath, showing ashes and bones in trays. This sight felt surreal, a stark departure from my memories of my dad.

Yet, at that moment, I realized my dad continues to exist in multiple realms. While my intellect may not comprehend Jack Thorne's words, "Those we love never truly leave us. There are things that death cannot touch." In my heart, I know it is true. I can feel it. My dad's spirit lives on within me. I can recall his gaze and smile at any moment, and remembering him brings a warm and heartfelt feeling. He transformed into something new, just like the cyclical rhythm of nature. I saw through his passing; what comes from the ground goes back to the ground. This expanded my understanding, and it was humbling. We all return to the embrace of the earth.

That day, my relationship with the earth's elements changed. It granted me a sense of closure—but only after I embraced all the realities presented to me. By being in the panoramic view of mourning, I saw grief as not just sadness; it could have joy too.

In grief, we can feel love and gratitude. In times of uncertainty, when we are lost, we need a space that allows us to acknowledge our discomfort while holding all parts of us together so that the old can transmute into the new, not by resistance, rejection, denial, or avoidance, but by gently embracing all that we encounter. My grief allowed me to see that my dad and I were not two anymore but one. Through his passing, I saw that we would never be apart. He is one with me in spirit.

Only from this way of seeing can you understand what the legendary martial artist Bruce Lee eloquently articulates:

> It is beyond intellectual knowing and cannot be grasped by the ordinary mind. When we awake to the realization that there is no barrier, and never has been, one realizes that one is everything—mountains, rivers, grasses, trees, sun, moon, stars, universe are all oneself. There is no longer a division between myself and others, no longer any feeling of alienation or fear. Realizing this results in true compassion. Other people and things are not seen as apart from oneself but, on the contrary, as one's own body.

Through this viewpoint, the illusion of separation, deeply rooted in our survival mind, dissolves in an instant. What often appears as a confounding problem presents its resolution simply when we change the way we see. What escapes our sight, and tricks us into thinking it's lost, missing, or far away, is never truly gone; it remains present, visible through the Heart Space.

When we bring our awareness into the Heart Space, we allow our mind to perceive what our heart can always see—a panoramic view of life, interconnected and constantly evolving. This viewpoint goes beyond time, space, distance, and linearity. Its inherent openness and capacity enable us to embrace life's paradoxes and navigate discomfort. We gain insight into our inner world and the world around us through the Heart Space.

Pema Chödrön, an American Tibetan Buddhist, captures the experience of connecting with our hearts and allowing them to be touched. She says, "You begin to discover that it's bottomless, that it doesn't have any resolution, that this heart is huge, vast, and limitless. You begin to discover how much warmth and gentleness is there, as well as how much space."

This place is innate in you. You are born with it. It is your home. Your biology even supports this. The heart is the first organ to form and function in a human embryo, not the brain. On a spiritual level, it serves as a sanctuary—a refuge for rest, where you can be yourself and live your life with both lightness and depth.

Some people have spent their entire lives searching for this kind of home but can never find it if they only look outside themselves. Sometimes, we perceive life as a linear journey that starts at one point and ends at another. But when you delve into the essence of the journey, it resembles more of a circle. You begin from where you are and return to it repeatedly. Perhaps that's why it's often said that the longest distance in the world is the journey from the head to the heart. This journey may seem to take forever as if you're making no progress. In a sense, it's true that you're going nowhere, for you're already home. You are never away from it. You simply need to go down 18 inches from your head.

WHEN THE HEART LEADS, THE MIND IS AT EASE

In the world of survival, knowing nothing is often perceived as unsafe and unacceptable, yet Socrates claims, "The only true wisdom is knowing that you know nothing." In the willingness to let go of what you know, you face the world with sincere humility and openness, for only when your heart cracks open do you begin living. That doesn't mean you abandon your intellectual capacity. It's a matter of intelligence shifting to the heart.

The mind can be at ease when it's free from the burden of constantly generating predictions, comparisons, and judgments and holding onto old stories. When our minds are cluttered with facts, ideas, rules, and expectations, it becomes challenging to perceive anything new. The true power of our minds lies not in accumulating knowledge but in creating a blank canvas where fresh thoughts and insights can paint their vivid strokes.

Sometimes, beautiful moments are beyond what our eyes can see or words can express. The highest truth can't be contained in this tiny brain of ours, but it can be universally felt through a receptive and open heart. Hellen Keller, a prolific author of the 20th century who became blind and deaf when she was a toddler, wrote, "The best and most beautiful things in the world cannot be seen, nor touched, but are felt in the heart." How true that is!

You experience the world not by what you see but by the way you see. When you see beauty and interconnectedness through the eye of your heart, lo and behold, the world seems more beautiful and whole. Even in grief, pain, and challenges, you'll see beauty too, for the world mirrors the heart. As Robert Sardello writes in *Heartfulness*, "We shape the world through the manner in which we receive the world into our hearts."

In a world characterized by opposing views and divisions —true vs. false, right vs. wrong, good vs. bad, you vs. me, us vs. them—we yearn for a space where differences can find common ground, even within ourselves. Just as a period in writing offers a brief interlude between sentences, our capacity to pause grants us the remarkable ability to craft a fresh narrative, one that transcends the constraint of our fragmented stories.

Our thoughts flow continuously, without commas or periods, creating an unbroken stream of words that interpret reality, label emotions, and analyze experiences. I encourage you to explore and uncover the metaphorical commas and periods concealed within the depths of your Heart Space—a momentary pause and relief from the constant need for definitive answers. By embracing the unknown, you will discover that your thoughts emerge from a deep and authentic place in harmony with your true essence.

REFLECTIONS AT YOUR OWN PACE

1. Reflect on the notion of a true encounter. How often do you truly engage your senses and fully connect with what is before you? Are there areas of your life where you could cultivate a more open and receptive approach?
2. This chapter suggests that the mind can be at ease when it doesn't hold onto old stories or constantly generate predictions, comparisons, and judgments. Reflect on the clutter in your mind, including opinions and expectations, and consider how it may hinder your ability to see or embrace new ideas. How can you create the space for fresh thoughts and insights to emerge?
3. Consider letting go of what you know and approach the world with humility and openness. How would this shift in perspective impact your experience of life? How would it affect your interactions with others?

SIX
THE HEART'S RELATIONAL INTELLIGENCE

We can only be said to be alive in those moments when our hearts are conscious of our treasures.

> THORNTON WILDER

Your life is full of hidden treasures. You may not believe me. But I hope you are willing to entertain this thought. Because what if it's true? What if it doesn't take much effort to discover the hidden treasures of your life other than the willingness to be open to them?

Rather than trying to convince you, I would like to help you see a glimpse of the extraordinary in the ordinary.

Ready?

I invite you to use your imagination while you read the next few paragraphs. Later, you can practice this exercise yourself in your own time.

Imagine . . .

From where you sit, look at the objects around you. Choose an object that comes to your attention.

For example, the fan on my ceiling caught my attention. It has hung there since we moved into our house over a decade ago, blending into the background unnoticed. But today, my gaze lingers on its shape and the generous layer of dust that has collected on it.

As I connect with this seemingly mundane object, a remarkable narrative of its origin unfolds before me. The raw materials were extracted from the depths of the Earth's core, where darkness and pressure reign. After undergoing meticulous processing, molding, and assembly, the object was carefully packaged for a long journey.

This unassuming object likely traveled greater distances than the average person on Earth. Its voyage began at the mining site and continued through the metal processing facility. From there, it progressed to the manufacturing plant, undergoing scrutiny and careful storage before embarking on a transoceanic expedition. After crossing vast seas, it briefly found refuge in a warehouse before gracing store shelves. Finally, it reached its ultimate destination—the ceiling of my living room.

The existence of this object is a testament to the contributions of a substantial number of individuals, potentially exceeding a couple of hundred: mining engineers, designers, manufacturing workers, transportation staff, dedicated shipping personnel, warehousing staff, diligent store employees, and, in the final act, my husband and me.

As I sit here, gazing upward, I envision with my mind's eye the cables, lights, and the flow of electricity converging to empower it to fulfill its role—as a fan.

In the hustle and bustle of the daily grind, who has time to even think about a fan, right? But, in a moment of deep observation, I am struck by the sheer magnificence of this ordinary everyday object. The once-neglected ceiling fan now unveils its extraordinary existence, connecting me to its origin and the vast network of people who contributed to its creation and journey. This awareness fills me with a sense of awe and deep appreciation for the intricate richness of its relational history.

When we take the time to truly look at something in a relational way, we can perceive far beyond what our eyes can see and what our autopilot, short-attention mind can comprehend.

Now, if gratitude, wonder, and appreciation can arise from an object we take for granted, imagine what a relational and panoramic view not bound by time and space can do for us.

YOU ARE A RELATIONAL BEING

The fabric of life is made of interconnected relationships. Nothing exists outside of a relationship—not a speck of dust, a fan, a bug, or the air we breathe. And most importantly, not you and me. From the moment of our conception to our final breath, our existence unfolds within relationships.

You and I were conceived through multi-faceted relationships. It began with the bond between two individuals, followed by the union of a particular egg and sperm within the womb, where we briefly found our place. Over the initial 41 weeks of our existence, we experienced an intimate connection with our mothers, encompassing the air, water, and sustenance she took in, along with her feelings and emotions. In return, our growth in the womb informed and affected our mothers too. Numerous studies on fetal-maternal microchimerism found that, long after a baby is born, the cells that migrate through the mother's bloodstream and circle back into the baby leave a permanent imprint in the mother's tissues, bones, brain, and skin.

The journey doesn't stop there. As we enter this world, we become an integral part of an expansive inter- and intra-relational network system that blurs the boundary between what's inside our skin and the world outside.

Your individual self is fundamentally an ecosystem. In fact, you are not 100% human. I am not kidding!

According to the latest research in microbiology, you are only 43% human. Approximately 57% of your body comprises bacteria, viruses, protozoa, and fungi. On average, an estimated 30 trillion human cells and 39 trillion microbial cells are in the adult human body. Your body isn't just you—it's filled with dynamic, diverse microbial communities that work symbiotically with your body to keep you alive and healthy. They communicate with your cells, train your immune system, fight infection, regulate your metabolism, affect your mood, and influence how much energy you burn. There is a universe living inside you. What makes you *you* is the interconnectedness of what is living in and outside of your body.

Let's press this point further. To be you, there must be the Earth, for you are made of her elements. About 99% of your body comprises oxygen, hydrogen, nitrogen, carbon, calcium, and phosphorus. To have all these vital elements, the entire ecosystem of the Earth must maintain its balance.

To be you, you must also have food to eat. That means there must be plants, land to grow your food, animals, insects, water, sunlight, and bacteria. There must be farmers and hundreds of thousands of people who grow and deliver your food supplies.

Ready to have your mind blown? For you to exist here and now, in this world, at least 4,096 humans had to exist over the span of 400 years!

2 parents,
4 grandparents,
8 great grandparents,
16 second great-grandparents,
32 third great-grandparents,
64 fourth great-grandparents,
128 fifth great-grandparents,
256 sixth great-grandparents,
512 seventh great-grandparents,
1,024 eighth great-grandparents,
2,048 ninth great-grandparents,
4,096 tenth great-grandparents.

You are the result of the lives of many people who lived before you. You wouldn't be here without them.

Your relational fabric is also woven into your identity. Who you are can't be described in isolation. For example, I became a mother because of my children; I would not have been a mother without their existence. Our identity is not fixed but relational. I am an author in relation to my readers. I am a Torontonian in regard to where I live and a coach in relation to my coaching clients. You can be a mother but also a manager in relation to the people you oversee or a consultant in relation to your client.

The way we communicate reflects our relational nature as well. Let's say you return home from a vacation and eagerly want to share your experience. Depending on who you talk to, you adapt your story and focus on a different aspect of your trip. You might share more intimate, personal experiences with close friends and general stories with your work colleagues.

Our sense of belonging is also relational. We include or exclude others by defining our relationship with them. As a result, our identity becomes remarkably fluid. It changes to accommodate the social context we use to define ourselves at any given time.

The fluidity of our identity becomes particularly evident during major sports events like the World Cup. Living in Toronto, one of the world's most culturally diverse cities, I've witnessed this phenomenon numerous times. Canadian-born soccer fans, for instance, often identify with their parents' heritage during the World Cup. I recall my time in the Little Portugal neighborhood, where residents celebrated Portugal's victories with great enthusiasm, proudly displaying Portuguese flags on their cars and homes. However, it's worth noting that these same individuals equally embrace their Canadian identity when our national hockey team competes on the international stage.

As relational beings, we possess remarkable flexibility in our sense of self and belonging. We are more fluid than we realize. In fact, we shapeshift every day depending on whom we interact with. Can you imagine what would be possible if we tap into this ability more consciously?

It would enable us to relate to others regardless of our differences. We can always discover shared common ground even when faced with stark disparities in ideology, religion, or opinion. This willingness to explore our relatedness bridges the "Me vs. You" and "We vs. Them" narratives and allows us to come together as "We *and* Us." After all, we share the same home: Earth.

On an individual level, many of us have confronted moments of crisis that have left us feeling adrift—whether due to job loss, relationship breakdowns, or significant life transitions. These experiences can shake our sense of self. However, recognizing the relational nature of our identity assures us that we never truly lose ourselves. Just as water remains inherently water regardless of the vessel it occupies, our core identity, our very essence, remains unchanged despite the challenges we face. With this understanding, we can find the freedom to channel our energy and attention toward nurturing relationships in the present moment.

Here is the truth that most people don't realize: you are indeed unique, but you cannot be unique alone. You are unique in relation to others. Like clapping, you can't make a sound with only one hand. It takes two to clap.

RELATIONAL FABRIC IN OUR LANGUAGE

The heart of our existence is entwined within the fabric of language, as is particularly evident in the structure of a simple sentence. A sentence comprises a subject, verb, and object. None of these elements can stand alone; their significance and meaning emerge through their interplay and relationships with one another.

Consider the sentence, "Jane throws a ball." Here, "Jane" is the subject, "throws" is the verb, and "ball" is the object.

Each component relies on the others to create a complete and coherent meaning. Without the subject, there would be no one to perform the action. Without the verb, there would be no action taking place. And without the object, there would be nothing being acted upon.

The dynamics of relationality extend far beyond the structure of a sentence. Even in a seemingly simple statement like "John is walking," hidden connections and implications are at play. Walking is more than the act of moving one's feet. For John to walk, he depends on the ground beneath him, forming a connection that offers stability and support with every step. Simultaneously, his body engages in a coordinated interplay of balance and muscular movements. John's ability to walk is influenced by factors that extend beyond his own existence, including his environment.

The relational connection between humans and their surroundings is even more prominent in Indigenous languages. For example, in the Passamaquoddy language, spoken in Eastern Maine and Western New Brunswick, the word "walk" changes based on the context.

Kisahqewse – One walks up the hill.
Motapewse – One walks down the hill.
Milawuhse – One walks into water.
Kcitawse – One walks far into it, like a forest or opening.
Ksokawse – One walks across something, like a road or stretch of forest.

You can see how these words, though all describing the act of walking, convey a different picture and feeling to the mind. The word "walk" is not separated from its relational context. Depending on the terrain and surface someone walks on, the word used paints different mental pictures and evokes various colors, textures, and landscapes. It even conveys a distinct manner in which a person moves their feet. Walking uphill, on ice, or through a wetland requires different adaptations to our movement. Here, we begin to see a panoramic picture of the otherwise mechanical and ordinary physical activity of moving one's feet from one spot to another.

The way we use language reflects a more profound truth about our lives. Every sentence, even the simplest one, contains hidden connections and relationships. By embracing this awareness, we can shift our perspective and see the world in a whole new way—one that goes beyond separation and isolation. This realization opens a new realm of possibilities where the mundane becomes extraordinary, and our comprehension of ourselves expands to include the profound interconnectedness of all things.

SHIFTING FROM NOUNS TO VERBS IN PERCEIVING THE WORLD

Now, I am sure you agree with me on this: our identities, perceptions, and experiences are not fixed entities. They represent an evolving and dynamic relationship between our inner and outer worlds.

In addition to Passamaquoddy, other North American Indigenous languages—including Cree, Ojibwe, and Mi'kmaq—offer a profound insight into the continuously evolving nature of this relationship. Unlike Spanish or French, which assign gender to nouns, these Indigenous languages categorize nouns as animate or inanimate. Instead of perceiving elements like rivers, trees, lands, rocks, waterfalls, or friends as fixed and unchanging, these cultures view them as verbs—constantly moving and always changing. In her book *Braiding Sweetgrass: Indigenous Wisdom, Scientific Knowledge, and the Teachings of Plants*, Robin Wall Kimmerer, an ecological scientist and member of the Potawatomi Nation, eloquently explains:

> A bay is a noun only if water is dead. When bay is a noun, it is defined by humans, trapped between its shores and contained by the word. But the verb *wiikwegamaa*—to be a bay—releases the water from bondage and lets it live. "To be a bay" holds the wonder that, for this moment, the living water has decided to shelter itself between these shores, conversing with cedar roots and a flock of baby mergansers. Because it could do otherwise—become a stream or an ocean or a waterfall, and there are verbs for that, too. To be a hill, to be a sandy beach, to be a Saturday, all are possible verbs in a world where everything is alive. Water, land, and even a day, the language a mirror for seeing the animacy of the world, the life that pulses through all things, through pines and nuthatches and mushrooms. This is the language I hear in the woods; this is the language that lets us speak of what wells up all around us.

A botanical researcher, Arthur Haines, gives another example of Robin Wall Kimmerer's quote. In a short reflection, he explains how learning an Indigenous language enriches his understanding and helps the students in his botany classes see the interconnectivity of botanical cycles, patterns, and structures. "In Passamaquoddy, there is no noun for field, it is a verb: *pomskute*—there is a field, a field extends along. It represents an understanding of how dynamic the landscape is, always changing from year to year."

As I immerse myself in the wisdom of Indigenous languages, a profound realization dawns on me. Those who hold these languages close to their hearts perceive trees, animals, and the forces of nature—such as wind, rain, and fire—as spirited beings. Their understanding of the world is rooted in deep connections and relationships.

When a tree ceases to be an object but is instead a living being, it opens a gateway for communication, inviting us to acknowledge the tree's ability to engage with us. In the presence of these vibrant spirits, communication can flow effortlessly as we listen to their silent whispers and honor their ever-changing expressions.

Through this relational awareness, we embark on a journey of discovering a richer way of relating—one that extends far beyond the boundaries of mere words and concepts. This authentic connection originates from the depths of our Heart Space, where true understanding and empathy reside.

Imagine what would be different if we shifted our perspective and began perceiving ourselves, others, and everything around us not as fixed and disconnected nouns but as verbs in constant expression, occurrence, and unfolding. How would such a shift impact the way we show up and respond to ourselves, others, and our environment?

TRANSCENDING FEAR AND SURVIVAL

As we delve into the deep, interconnected web of relationships, we begin to realize how life supports and sustains us on many levels. This web reminds us that we are not alone but rather essential parts of a whole; much larger than ourselves.

Perhaps we can borrow the perspective of Leland Melvin, an American astronaut who spent 213 days in space. When asked to share an aha moment from space that changed his perspective of the world, he described having a meal with French, German, and Russian astronauts at 17,500 miles per hour while listening to Sade's "Smooth Operator." He said:

> I look out the window, and I see the planet again. We're going around it so fast and we're coming over Virginia. I look down and I'm thinking, "My parents are probably having a meal." Five minutes later, we're over Paris, where Léo's from, our French long-duration astronaut. And then Yuri, from Russia, can look over to the side and see his home.
>
> And so, in this one little moment in time, we're looking at our respective homes, breaking bread, and celebrating like we are in space. And that's when this shift happened, because I saw so much of the planet in 90 minutes. I saw all these different things happening. And that's when I think I really got my over-perspective. I thought it would be when I did this task of installing the Columbus laboratory, but that paled in comparison to the human piece of us sharing and breaking bread and seeing the planet in that way. Our respective homes, up in space.

That moment of panoramic relationality changed him. It

is beyond intellectual knowledge, but it resulted in a profound shift in consciousness.

I am not an astronaut and have never been to outer space. But I had an ordinary yet profound aha moment right here on Earth.

One day, I took a short walk between virtual meetings to get fresh air. I felt stuck. My work was not fulfilling anymore. I didn't feel like I belonged. I knew it was time to move on, but I did not know how. My heart felt heavy with silent frustration and sadness.

It was early summer, and the little park I visited was full of lush green grass. I walked to an open field. Looking down, I watched my feet move one at a time. Suddenly, what seemed obvious became remarkable to me. I realized that with every step, the ground held up my feet. It didn't matter which direction I took; it was always there, ready to receive, ready to support in a way so ordinary that my mind took it for granted. Even when I fell, the ground would never fail to catch me.

At that moment, I felt my burden lifted. My body let go of its tension. I felt open and relaxed. My breathing became effortless. I released the need to carry my own weight. As this new insight arose, my survival mind let go of its need for control.

I saw the illusion of my mental construct—the construct that made me believe I had to take the "right" step, for if I made a wrong step, I would crash to the ground, and nothing would hold me.

Rather than seeing the ground as vast, alive, encompassing, and connected with me, I only saw myself, alone with vague dark patches ahead that I had yet to figure out. How naïve and arrogant is the ego mind?

This moment made me realize there is no wrong step; there is only *a* step. I am free to step in any direction because, like the ground, life is larger than me. Anywhere I go, any direction I take, I am being supported.

As understanding informed and permeated through my body, I removed my summer shoes and gently closed my eyes. Lifting my foot, I walked, releasing my reliance on eyesight, savoring the sensation that I felt when the bottom of my foot touched the ground. In this moment of connectivity, another insight emerged. When we think we are stuck, going nowhere, even when we lock ourselves in a room inside our house, we still move long distances without having to do anything.

Do you know why?

The Earth rotates on its axis at 1,037 miles per hour (1,670 km) and orbits the sun at 67,000 miles per hour (107,000 km). Simultaneously, the solar system travels through the Milky Way at an average velocity of 448,000 miles per hour (720,000 km). Finally, the Milky Way moves through the universe at approximately 2,237,000 miles per hour. Because you are on the Earth, you are moving with it, for no matter where you run or hide, you will always remain on the Earth's rounded surface.

This realization would not have come to me if I had been unwilling to escape my rigid mental construct, unwilling to slow down, and be present as I walked. Like Leland Melvin's moment, my fresh encounter with the ground shifted my consciousness.

Fast forward, the panoramic view of relationality that I experienced allowed me to leave a 20-year corporate career and follow my heart's path. I learned what it meant to move one step at a time with the unwavering trust that the ground beneath me will always be there. To face uncertainty with a different kind of certainty. The ground is real, it's not my easily doubted, narrow, limited, and depending-on-the-weather survival mind. The ground represents a universal relational web that holds me—its existence and nature doesn't depend on what I think. Just like the sun doesn't suddenly stop showing up because I am mad at it or because I have a dreadful day. Thank goodness!

The panoramic view of relationality widens the aperture of our consciousness, giving us a more encompassing, multidimensional view of who we are in our ever-evolving living connection to the world. In relationality, we can experience flow and lightness. As Fr. Richard Rohr says, "To live in such a way is to live inside of an unexplainable hope because your life will now feel much larger than your own. In fact, it is not your own life, and yet, paradoxically, you are more 'you' than ever before."

Deep within our wholeness resides an unshakable sense of safety that we cannot access when we are in the survival mind. The relational nature of you and me provides the interface for possibilities, transcends feelings of isolation, and unearths a profound sense of belonging.

Through the relational way of being and seeing, we can fully understand what Heraclitus, the 500 BC Greek philosopher, proclaimed: "The only constant in life is change." As we cultivate relational awareness of the Heart Space, we embark on a path of living and embodying the dynamic nature of constant change, being fluid in the face of complexity.

REFLECTIONS AT YOUR OWN PACE

1. How does acknowledging that your body contains not only human cells but also a diverse ecosystem of microbial life affect your perception of self? How does this recognition of yourself as an interconnected ecosystem with multiple intelligent elements shape your understanding of your own existence?
2. Reflect on the ancestral connections that have contributed to your existence. How does recognizing the lives of those who came before you and their impact on your being enrich your understanding of yourself?
3. Reflect on moments of crisis or significant life transitions that have challenged your sense of self. How does recognizing your core identity as inherently relational provide a sense of stability and resilience in times of change? How can you leverage this understanding to navigate future challenges with greater ease?

SEVEN
LIVING IN DISCOVERY

Man cannot discover new oceans unless he has the courage to lose sight of the shore.

ANDRÉ GIDE

Imagine trekking through the rugged South African terrain alongside Boyd Varty, a seasoned lion tracker raised in the Londolozi Game Reserve. Varty shares his story as a lion tracker and the timeless wisdom unearthed from this ancient art in his captivating book, *The Lion Tracker's Guide to Life*. Lion trackers undertake their mission by traversing trails, dirt roads, watering holes, and riverbanks, meticulously deciphering clues to trace elusive lion pride. They use all their senses to decode the environment to accomplish this. A lion tracker must immerse themselves in what Varty calls the "following state." He defines this state as a constant, creative response to what is occurring. According to him, a tracker doesn't need to know everything; they just need to develop tracker awareness. Varty emphasizes, "As a tracker, our part is to be awake. Our part is to listen."

The trail often diverges into multiple paths, prompting the trackers to align their movements with the animals to choose the right course. He elaborates on his fellow tracker's approach:

> I watch as he lets the lion into his body. He begins to adopt the cadence of the track. He picks up speed as he walks to match the lion's steps. He allows the intelligence of his body to mirror the movements of the lion, and in this way, he enters a kind of resonance with the animal.

Tracking a living, moving being demands a constant connection. The trail acts as an invisible tether linking the tracker with the animal. In a profound state of presence devoid of judgment, assumptions, or expectations, the tracker becomes fully immersed in the interplay between themselves, the trail, and the animal. They sense the animal's temperament, speed, behavior, and the rhythm of its movement. The tracker, the lion, and the trail fuse into a harmonious unfolding, drawing the tracker along through the life force pulsating within the trail.

The trail they follow isn't always clear. Sometimes, what starts as a clear track becomes invisible. Paradoxically, Varty asserts, "Going down a path and not finding a track is part of finding the track. No action is considered a waste. The key is to keep moving, readjusting, and welcoming feedback." He adds, "Losing the track is not the end of the trail, but rather a space of preparation. The whole process is contained here as pure potentiality. Prepare yourself to hear the call and invite the unknown. Look for the first track, tune into the instrument of the body. All of these dynamics must lie latent in you as you look for the next track."

A tracker is absolutely committed to finding the wild animal yet does not allow that commitment to become a burden. They immerse themselves in a state of play and flow.

Navigating the wilderness and facing the unknown is not easy. Here's an account depicting a pivotal moment for Varty and his companions when they encountered a trail branching into multiple paths:

> It's hard to know when to stay on a trail and when to divert. It's hard to know when the lesson is to persist. And when the lesson is to let go, I think of all the angst I have felt between choices. I've been paralyzed by options, and the idea that there is a single right way. Renias (his fellow tracker) is more Zen. For him, the only choice is the one he has made. He knows any choice will set something in motion. This is the magic of the bush and life. You use your intention. Take action and let go.

Reflecting on this insight, he shares, "The Bush teaches us that the lesson is more about discovery than being correct. On the trail, there is not one way. The only mistake is to not make any choice, as it is in life."

I am drawn to Varty's story because it is a perfect example of being on a journey of discovery. Most aspects of our lives are predictable. Every day, we go to the same office, live in the same house, drive on the same roads, and work with the same people. Even without going anywhere, we can access information about tomorrow's weather. Wherever we go, we have access to a map to find the best route to our destination and obtain remarkably accurate travel times. All the information we need is just a click away. We've grown accustomed to the comfort of knowing what lies ahead before it unfolds.

From a very young age, we are raised to follow society's agenda of achievement. From kindergarten to university, we have a set of criteria to follow. These criteria and the subsequent curriculum and methodology have been tested to ensure they can equip people to contribute to the economy and society. The path is well-charted, offering a sense of predictability and security.

Throughout these formative years, we are taught how to *do*, not how to *be*. We are taught the known, not the unknown.

No wonder we are so attracted to books, blog posts, and courses with bombastic titles, such as "Seven Ways to Achieve Happiness," "Three Ways of Guaranteed Weight Loss," "The Big Secret to Awakening Your Superpower." We are drawn to systematic, proven, step-by-step ways of doing things. We are taught the result is what matters.

That is how our brains have been wired. They crave predictability. The certainty of external circumstances equals control. That is what we know best, and it feels safe.

But how often have we tried to apply these formulas for success and failed or felt utterly unfulfilled? Why is that?

Because we are using our "how to *do*" skill to find the "how to *be* "answer.

In survival, the best strategy to survive, compete, and

maintain dominance involves accumulation. Within the business arena, power increases in direct proportion to one's access to a wealth of data and information. In society, social influence is obtained by aligning with the in-group and mastering the accumulation of wealth. Even on social media, the game is to accumulate followers.

Moreover, in self and spiritual development, seekers often believe that growth requires the accumulation of more knowledge. If you read one more book, listen to yet another expert, take an additional course, or acquire more techniques, you will eventually unearth the answer you seek and realize your purpose in this world.

Perhaps focusing on accumulation has served you well. But if you've read this book up to this point, I am certain you are looking for something different. Because you know this:

More knowledge
doesn't mean more wisdom.

More success
doesn't mean more happiness.

More options
don't mean more freedom.

More doing
doesn't mean more productivity.

More time
doesn't mean more accomplishment.

You know there must be another way.
And you are right.

BEING IN DISCOVERY

Through helping my coaching clients and my own journey of self-discovery, one thing has become clear: the journey has no end. Understanding yourself and the world around you is a constant process. This form of knowledge doesn't come from accumulating information but from expanding your awareness of what *is*. It doesn't arise from rearranging what you know but from keeping your heart and mind open so that new and fresh insights can enter your awareness.

While learning may seem similar to discovery, it is fundamentally different. The root of learning lies in "earn," signifying the acquisition of something. It makes sense to acquire something when you don't have it or don't have enough. On the other hand, discovery is an action or process of uncovering something, implying the revelation of what is already present. Being in discovery allows you to flow with life, accepting change and growth as they naturally unfold.

When you begin your morning believing you must earn something, you wake up with a burden of responsibility on your shoulders. Your day might feel like a race rather than living. But when you view your day as another day of discovery, you wake up with a sense of lightness, with a little more excitement and curiosity about what today will bring.

Being in discovery is similar to the act of listening. All that's needed for listening is your presence. It's like tuning in to the world around you without the need to create or manufacture anything. Whether it's the bark of a dog, the hum of a passing car's engine, the rustling of leaves, or the sound of someone's voice, you simply receive it as it comes to you. In many ways, listening is far simpler than thinking because it doesn't require you to generate thoughts; instead, it allows you to absorb the richness of what already exists.

But you and I know that listening is hard to do. Our societal conditioning often emphasizes constant action as the primary means of gaining knowledge and achieving our goals. As a result, we struggle to listen and be receptive to what others say. This challenge extends even to our ability to listen to ourselves! Instead of fully absorbing what is being said, we feel compelled to formulate immediate responses.

What if we took a different approach? What if we released the need to always form opinions and formulate answers? Imagine the possibilities if we set aside our agenda and wholeheartedly immersed ourselves in the act of listening and discovery.

One summer, when my daughter was in kindergarten, we strolled through a nearby park. Above us, the sky painted a clear, vivid blue, with the summer sun reigning high during the equinox. A flock of birds soared in an elegant loop above us. My daughter broke the silence and asked, "Mommy, why don't the birds in the sky fall to the ground when they stop flapping their wings?"

Her question surprised me. I was impressed by the innate intelligence behind it. This intelligence didn't come from being taught the law of gravity or how to think. No, it stemmed from her inherent childlike wonder, keen observation, and curiosity about the world around her. She posed the question in response to her newfound discovery.

My gaze became fixed on one of the birds. Birds fly. Sometimes, they flap their wings; other times, they glide. Time froze for a moment, as if I were one with the bird, sensing the breeze cradling my feathers and lifting me as I soared through the sky. The next moment, an answer came to me. I said to her, "Well, it's because the air beneath their wings supports and holds them, allowing them to keep soaring up in the sky."

While my response may not be scientific, it did satisfy my daughter's curiosity. Thankfully, she didn't pose the typical follow-up questions most five-year-olds do. This encounter made me realize that, despite birds appearing to depend solely on their own efforts to fly, they are constantly and invisibly supported. The very essence of air lends its hand to their graceful flight.

Contemplating this experience, I've come to realize how our modern life conditions us to have a narrow depth of field that is only good for taking selfies. Me, me, and more me. Me and myself. Me and my issues. Me and what I think should happen. Me and my effort.

While we try to look outward to fulfill what we believe we lack inside, this narrow depth of field keeps the foreground and background focus blurred. Despite our best efforts, we cannot see the available resources and the invisible force that supports us. To be in a state of discovery, we must allow our inner witness to bring to light the superficial layers of our narratives and the self-imposed barriers we construct to maintain a sense of control.

Each of us has a witnessing capacity—the intangible

essence that allows us to be conscious of our thoughts, passing judgment, and emotions. Without our capacity to witness, how can we come to know our thoughts and feelings? As Mark Matousek describes, "The Witness is not an identity, not a separate self that lurks inside the mind or body. It is neither subject nor object. Instead, it's the omnipresent beingness that operates within all of us."

Tapping into our capacity to witness clears the path for wisdom, intuition, inspiration, and creativity to flow naturally. This process is never achieved through strenuous effort but, rather, through allowing these qualities to arise and come into our awareness. You see, allowing is not passive. It's an active, conscious decision that demands your intellect to trust the process and not resist whatever comes your way. It's not a weak decision either, for it calls for a body-mind-spirit understanding that all force is within you and works together with you.

The survival mind can't comprehend this way of being. To fully embody it, you must begin by adopting the encompassing and relational view of the Heart Space. This enables you to engage your witnessing capacity while holding the angst of the survival mind.

The practice of witnessing and allowing is simpler than you might think. Imagine the relief you would feel if you didn't have to constantly fix or change things but simply allowed them to be. We have just forgotten how to do it. As Bruno Barnhart, a Camaldolese monk, reveals in his contemplation, "The problem with us human beings is that we prefer a manageable complexity to an unmanageable simplicity." As our awareness deepens, our understanding of reality expands. Instead of busily concocting ideas in our heads, we create a sanctuary that allows us to witness an unfolding reality.

ABUNDANCE IN EVERYDAY MOMENTS: A LESSON FROM AN APRICOT TREE

My neighbor's backyard boasts a young apricot tree, its towering branches extend slightly into my yard. This morning, while I penned this paragraph, my attention was drawn to the mouthwatering, bright, luscious orange apricots adorning the branches that dared to trespass into my domain. These fruits had ripened almost to perfection, tempting me to sample their sweetness. I grabbed a short ladder parked against the opposite wall of my modest yard and positioned it near the tree. With excitement bubbling inside me, I ascended the ladder and plucked those radiant fruits. A moment of deep gratitude washed over me as I cradled them in my palms.

Is this what it is like to live in abundance? I wondered. To obtain these fruits, I had to do nothing other than be right next to where they grew, happen to notice them, and allow my desire to move me, grab the ladder, and pick the fruits. "Happen to notice" is key because I could have been preoccupied with thoughts and desires for other things that were "not here," such as an apple tree, or wishing I was on a sunny vacation on a tropical island instead of being "here," completely overlooking the abundance around me.

This experience made me realize the extent of our disconnection from nature. While wild birds and other animals live and get their food directly from the source for free, we must earn money to pay for our food and shelter. Therefore, we lack the direct experience and awareness of what it feels like to be nurtured by the bountiful force of nature that freely supports us and has a life of its own.

When you grow plants outdoors, some may require watering and fertilizing, yet most thrive without intervention. We need not fret over how they will grow or which branches will bear fruit; nature follows its course, regardless of our involvement. However, our struggle lies in attuning ourselves to nature's flow and engaging in the reciprocal exchange that sustains the entire system, where we are integral participants rather than mere outsiders.

By embracing life with a perspective of interconnectedness, we find an effortless rhythm imprinted within us. It's as simple as connecting and remaining open to the flow of available information. In doing so, our relational intelligence comes alive, revealing insights through heightened awareness. This powerful form of knowledge and intelligence doesn't come from being active but, rather, from being receptive.

Back to Varty's story, lion trackers are indeed active participants. They take action, but the difference is they put themselves in the process of discovery. Rather than *making* things happen, they *allow* things to happen. They listen. Their moves and progress are a response to the unfolding moments and revelations.

Consider, for instance, when Varty describes his fellow lion tracker:

> In a vast wilderness, 360 degrees of wild terrain, all he needs is the next first track, and then the next first track, and then the next first track, and the next first track. And he's able to

dial down the infinite possibilities of where that animal could have gone to a moment of knowing and a moment of presence . . . And all he needs is that next sign. So he doesn't know where it's going, but he knows how to get there: the next moment of presence.

Varty believes the moment of presence holds this whole model together. It contains:

The ability to slow down and continuously reflect and contemplate and be aware enough to know how your body is speaking. Be aware enough to know what's bringing you to life, be aware enough to know when you've lost the track. Be aware enough to know what the next small step is to take. If you are doing all of that consistently, what you are doing is you're committing to allowing the process to unfold.

He then says, "When you are doing that, the most incredible thing happens: you become so energized by the process itself that, at a certain point, it doesn't even matter whether you find that animal or not."

He provided a perfect yet ordinary example of being completely in tune with one's natural self. The trackers are free to listen, explore, and respond, drawing from a deep, interconnected intelligence within themselves. Their actions are never one-sided or carried out in isolation; instead, they are influenced by their ongoing discoveries. They remain attuned to the evolving relationship between themselves, the landscape, and the animals they seek. This interaction encompasses the interplay between what they know and don't know. In this flow, they are free to be themselves, unburdened by internal pressures or expectations.

There is no better way to face complexity and uncertainty than immersing ourselves in the unfolding process of discovery. Joy, delight, surprise, new ideas, creativity, and growth thrive where knowing meets the unknown. As we become more aware, we begin to see the constantly evolving world around us, filled with opportunities waiting to be uncovered.

Our Head Space starts from lack—an uncomfortable void yearning to be filled with something, anything. In contrast, our Heart Space originates from a wellspring of abundance, as if everything we need is already present, unfolding naturally before our eyes. Our role, then, becomes one of allowing, and granting this abundance the chance to be witnessed. It invites us to move in harmony with life rather than resist it.

Are you willing to trust the intelligence that works in all things?

After all, there is "us" in "tr*us*t." Trust is the foundation upon which all strong relationships are built. Life is not a lone journey. It is a journey of togetherness.

REFLECTIONS AT YOUR OWN PACE

1. How can the notion of "being in discovery" alter your perception of uncertainty and change in life?
2. How does listening and being receptive to your inner voice and intuition impact your decision-

making and overall well-being? How can you nurture your inner witness in your daily life?
3. How might you liberate yourself from the compulsion to control every aspect of your life and, instead, embrace the transformative power of allowing things to unfold naturally? What inner shifts or practices can you explore to cultivate a deeper sense of trust and surrender to the unfolding journey?

EIGHT
THE POWER OF BEING

The trick in life is not to try to get to be "happy," get to be "secure," get to be "content," but to start out being happy, being secure, being content, and go from there in the living of our daily lives.

NEALE DONALD WALSCH

Meet Kenichi Kanazawa, the Japanese artist who wields a magician's touch, turning the ordinary into the extraordinary. Kanazawa blends science and art with only three humble tools—a steel plate, a rubber mallet, and a bucket of sand—making the invisible visible before our eyes.

First, Kanazawa scatters sand onto a barren steel tabletop. Then, using a rubber mallet, he gently strokes the edge of the tabletop. As the mallet caresses the table's periphery, sound vibrations ripple through the steel, causing the sand to burst into a mesmerizing dance of chaos. This initial chaotic frenzy eventually harmonizes into captivating geometric patterns.

Each time he employs a mallet of a different size, the sand liberates itself from its prior formation and comes together into a new arrangement, as if imbued with a life of its own. This captivating art form is known as cymatics art.

The term "cymatics" was coined by Hans Jenny when he discovered a method to visualize sounds through their vibrations. His pioneering work, conducted from 1958 to 1972, aimed to capture the impact of sound on various media. Jenny's research unveiled that these effects weren't merely chaotic disruptions, they revealed dynamic and organized patterns resulting from the interaction between sound and matter.

As I contemplate Kanazawa's work, I can't help but think that in our survival trance, we resemble someone attempting to control grains of sand, painstakingly placing each one where we want it to be, all by hand. Imagine how laborious that process is! All because we remain unaware of the invisible principle that unifies all parts into a cohesive whole.

Our thoughts, emotions, sensations, perceptions, and behaviors are the grains of sand dancing, moving, and oscillating in resonance with the steel plate of our being. The sense of internal order and safety we seek doesn't come from being in control of our environment but from being in harmonious resonance with who we are. When we align with our true self, we can sense it. Feel it. Our body knows it.

We have greater capacity in the immaterial plane than in the material plane. Our intention, attention, inspiration, aspiration, thoughts, will, and drive are non-matter, invisible to the eyes. Yet, they can be felt, witnessed, and experienced. In our lives, we often encounter experiences that can be challenging to comprehend. Love, courage, compassion, conviction, commitment, resilience, patience, joy, curiosity, and creativity are not "things." You can't acquire these qualities by obtaining an object you desire. They come from being exactly who you are.

This means that, regardless of any circumstances, you, the one who is aware, can decide who you want to be at any given moment. You don't have to try hard because being yourself happens naturally, moment by moment.

In the world of scarcity, it makes sense to hold onto something as long as you can; otherwise, you might lose it. But the natural world doesn't work that way. You can't overeat now to prevent getting hungry later, nor can you hold your breath long enough to remove the need to breathe for the next few minutes. As Jesus once advised, "Do not worry about tomorrow, for tomorrow will worry about itself. Each day has enough trouble of its own." If only we were aware that life takes shape through our way of being, moment by moment.

EMBRACING OUR CAPACITY TO *BE* WITHOUT REASONS

For a long time, I used to believe that my ability to love relied on the qualities of others and the reasons behind why I loved them. It could be because of their appearance, how they treated me, their talents, or their significance in my life.

Then one day, a young black tuxedo cat appeared in our backyard. Evidently, it had visited multiple times because my daughter recognized and fed it right away. I, however, paid no attention and held no interest. I am not really a cat person or a fan of pets.

However, when she returned and approached me a few

days later, my attention shifted to her and our eyes met. I perceived her presence: a beautiful creature cloaked in fur. To my surprise, I began to caress her back and gaze at her affectionately. With no thought running through my mind, I felt love radiating from me to her. It was simply a tender, loving moment.

I had no reason to love that cat. Yet, a spontaneous expression welled up within me, much like a flashlight shining its glow outward. This light didn't originate from the cat; it emanated from within me. Love, which I once believed was generated from the "outside," had come from the "inside" all along. Through the love I projected on her, I noticed what a beautiful being she was. She ended up becoming our family's cat.

In this ordinary moment, I realized that our capacity to love is innate within us. Our Head Space often generates convincing reasons why we should or shouldn't feel good or why someone deserves love or not. When we feel the need to justify every aspect of life, this compulsion exerts control over us. We may come to believe that our inherent capacity depends on external conditions. In other words, we've deluded ourselves into making the world a cause for our state of being; for instance, because he is kind to me, I am nice to him. When he is rude to me, he doesn't deserve my affection. Because I've made a big mistake, I don't deserve to be happy. Not until I lose some weight, can I feel good about myself.

Oh, how everything becomes so conditional! When we give our power and freedom away to our external environment, it governs our moods, feelings, and responses. Without realizing it, we've signed up for a victim game that we can never win. In a way, we've been misusing one of our mightiest tools: our intellectual and rational mind. It doesn't serve the truth. It serves what you believe and can find any reason under the sky to support whatever you think is true.

If you have a good reason to love someone or feel happy, courageous, and confident, that's wonderful! But how often do these feelings dissipate when your circumstances change? It's as though our mood and self-worth are at the mercy of the unpredictable emotional climate, leaving us often hanging by a thread.

Yet, we are all free to love, to be courageous, happy, and confident without needing reasons. We've all experienced this when the moment is just right, and our thoughts no longer hold us captive. When was the last time you experienced such freedom?

Many people share with me that they feel most peaceful, connected, and calm when they spend time in nature. One person in my facilitation group shared her reason: "Because I can be myself among the trees." I suggested this happens because she let the trees be trees and herself be herself among the trees.

In such moments, we release ourselves from the weight of expectations, a burden we often carry in our interactions with others. When we walk in nature, we experience a pure sense of connection and inner peace, free from the need for justification. This feeling exists, undisturbed, until we reintroduce our worries and concerns back into our minds.

Once upon a time, a student approached his teacher, who was meditating under a willow tree. The young man said, "Teacher, I've been practicing patience, kindness, and positivity for months, and my life has improved. I feel better and have more peace."

He continued, "But, three days ago, while I was on my way to my cousin's wedding, my bag with all my money and personal belongings got stolen. It's been very discouraging and difficult to feel centered after the incident. Even as I talk to you, I feel defeated and quite angry."

"I know it's not the end of the world, but I'm still shocked and can't sleep at night. Do you have any advice to help me focus and have peace of mind?"

Slowly, the teacher opened his eyes, moved his head towards his student, and looked at him compassionately.

He said, "My dear, from your story, I conclude the thief only took your bag and belongings, not your peace of mind. You can bring your peace back once you finish mourning your loss. The peace is still in you. No thief can steal it, except if you think they can."

Love, peace, and good feelings often associated with achieving your desires don't come from external sources. They originate within you, ever-present, unlike the clothes you buy that can wear out, the status or the possessions you earn that others can take away from you.

While this concept may be challenging to grasp, our conditioning often leads us to believe that everything, even happiness, should have a reason. Yet, when you were a child, you possessed all these qualities without the need to earn them. Do you know why? Because you were not preoccupied with reasons. You were free to simply *be*.

You have the power to summon and radiate these inner qualities. Think of it like tuning an analog radio: initially, there might be static, represented by doubts and overthinking when you try to connect with these qualities. But with practice, you refine your inner tuning, reducing the interference. Just as adjusting the radio dial allows you to find the music you seek, tuning into your Heart Space helps you discover the emotional and mental states you desire. Like Kenichi Kanazawa's cymatics art, the grains of thought, feeling, action, and desire oscillate in harmony with your being. Without realizing it, your outer circumstances will naturally align with you.

This process of inner tuning and resonance demonstrates that creating a fulfilling life is not about external circumstances but about understanding the depths of your own being.

WHO AM I?

Kabir Helminski, in his book *Living Presence*, asserts that "Being is the integrity of everything." He emphasizes that "Without Being, our activity becomes chaotic, delinquent, purposeless, and wasteful." Helminski firmly believes that "Being is the reservoir of possibilities, the creative energy that propels our actions," He contends that "Being is the domain of quality. Whatever we do with Being embodies qualities and attributes more purely and intensely" and concludes that "We can bring quality into the details of life if we remember to be and act with precision."

Through your Being, you express who you are. Yet, in today's materialistic and competitive society, staying authentic can be challenging, given the societal and workplace pressures that often promote conformity. Gabor Maté, a renowned expert in addiction and trauma, emphasizes the significance of embracing our genuine selves despite these strong social pressures and expectations. In a candid interview, Maté succinctly puts it, "The question is not changing who we are. It's a question of becoming who we are." This insight, stemming from his extensive research, patient work, and prolific writings on trauma, reveals that people can undergo remarkable transformations and healing when they reconnect with themselves, even when dealing with significant illness. He asserts that this process of becoming who we are is a fundamental human need.

However, let's engage in an experiment to test how easily your Head Space can grasp your essence. To aid this exploration, I invite you to reflect on these questions:

Without your mind, who are you?

*Without your pain, achievements,
distractions, challenges,
history, and ambitions,
who remains?*

As you contemplate these inquiries, you may begin to sense the limitations of your logical mind in providing a definitive answer. I bet no matter how intelligent or persistent you are, you won't find a satisfying response. The hard truth? Your Head Space will never be able to grasp your essence because your being is not an abstraction; it is a living presence, ever pulsating and vibrating with life's energy.

Trying to intellectually encapsulate the essence of your being is like attempting to capture a fleeting moment in a photograph. Just as you think you have captured it, the moment slips away, replaced by the next, leaving behind a trail of infinite moments that are impossible to capture and contain. The more you seek to confine and define your being, the more it slips through your fingers.

Our mind loves to create stories so much that we *become* the stories we tell ourselves. "I am my achievement. I am my failure. I am my success, I am the hassle I am trying to improve." However, when a dominant story no longer appears coherent, we feel uneasy, like a toddler losing their beloved teddy bear. The stories we tell ourselves become our gravity and reason for being in this world. Without them, we don't know what to do and how to be.

Do you see the mind game at play here? Without the story of your identity and survival, the part of you that craves constant vigilance, control, and the pursuit of fixing and perfecting is rendered jobless. Similar to a worker whose job security is in jeopardy. The survival mind has a strong motivation to keep you preoccupied with anticipating problems that might occur in the future and concocting regrets about the past.

Our Head Space is wired to notice movement and distinctions. It's like when we observe a moving object against a stationary background; our attention naturally focuses on the object in motion rather than the static backdrop. Likewise, in our inner experience, we tend to focus on the constant flux of our thoughts, feelings, and sensations. Yet, within us, there exists an unchanging presence that transcends the fleeting nature of these observable fluctuations.

Rupert Spira offers some insight worth considering. He says:

I am that which knows or is aware of all experience, but I am not myself an experience. I am aware of thoughts but am not myself a thought; I am aware of feelings and sensations but am not myself a feeling or sensation; I am aware of perceptions but am not myself a perception. Whatever the content of the experience, I know or am aware of it.

These words invite us to contemplate that our true essence is the knowing awareness behind our experiences, distinct from the ever-changing content of our inner worlds.

You can relate this concept to the experience of watching a movie. You can become so absorbed in a scene that you feel what the characters are feeling. You laugh, cry, or become tense as the story unfolds. Yet, you allow yourself to experience it all because you know it is just a movie, a form of entertainment. Behind the sound effects and convincing storyline, you know, without a doubt, that you will be okay no matter what happens. The screen where the images are projected remains unchanged, and you, as the viewer, remain yourself.

Similarly, the deepest part of our nature is unbreakable, unaltered, and as unchanging as the movie screen. Regardless of the events and fluctuations that occur in our everyday lives, this immutable aspect of our being remains constant and resilient.

Therefore, we need a way of holding both aspects. On one hand, we acknowledge the bodily sensations of our existential angst, the discomfort we feel within ourselves. These sensations are real and require our acceptance. On the other hand, we must recognize and embrace the unchangeable nature of our essence. As the observer, you can watch how your mind assigns meanings to these feelings, while acknowledging the deeper awareness that remains untouched by these passing sensations.

In this context, love achieves its ultimate fulfillment through the simple act of witnessing. For love to be fully realized, it must be given and received. Your aliveness, thoughts, emotions, and sensations find solace in the arms of a non-judgmental presence, where they are seen and accepted. As Parker Palmer wisely states, "The human soul doesn't want to be advised, fixed, or saved. It simply wants to be witnessed exactly as it is."

You come to a full circle when you realize that the validation, acceptance, and love you seek outside must be found within. The piece that you think is missing is always within you. You are the one that you have been waiting for all your life. The love, acceptance, and validation you give yourself are directly proportional to your ability to love and accept others as they are. As a relational, interconnected being, inside you are the whole world. When you witness and heal yourself, you are healing our collective existence.

Your journey is to discover and experience your true, un-theoretical, and un-mechanical self that moves and evolves within the relational web around you.

And as you progress, let Mary S. Watt's words remind you:

Is it an effort for Life to be alive?
Is it a struggle for Consciousness to be conscious?
Is it strange for Mind to be intelligent?
Is it difficult for Love to be loving?

Neither is it a struggle for you to be what you already are.

Perhaps it's too simple for your conditioned mind to let go of the belief that you must work hard to become who you want to be. But you see, you can't achieve what you already are. It can only be realized. Kabir Helminski shared his definition of "realization." He writes, "In its fullest meaning, is not merely knowing something, but making it real in oneself."

The way to make it real is by recognizing the fullness of who you are. The secret lies in embracing each moment as it unfolds. Can you be kind, confident, or courageous for a moment? Can you express generosity, compassion, or love for a moment? Be productive for a moment. Can you surrender, be joyful, or be playful for a moment? Yes, you can. After all, time is a continuous presence. Past and future are constructs of the mind, tools for comprehending complex data. Beyond thinking lies the capacity to feel, sense, and imagine. Beyond thought is another level of being. When you approach life from this place, you'll find yourself more alive, free, and grounded. You are here to express your being.

What are you radiating in the world?

REFLECTIONS AT YOUR OWN PACE

1. Reflect on a time when discomfort or pain became a source of strength and growth. How did you navigate that experience, and what did you learn about yourself? How does witnessing and acknowledging your own experiences equate to love and acceptance?

2. Can you think of a time when you felt witnessed and accepted exactly as you are? In what ways have you discovered the power and significance of self-validation, self-acceptance, and self-love? How does this internal validation impact your relationship with yourself and others?
3. Recall a moment when you experienced love or peace without any specific reason. How did it feel to be in that state, free from the need to justify or rationalize it? How can you cultivate more of these moments in your life?

NINE
RADICAL RECEPTIVITY

When we expand our observation to include not only our thoughts and opinions but also our inner states and feelings, our whole perception of reality changes, resulting in different actions, feelings, and interventions.

RIA BAECK

Did you know that in English, the words "Earth" and "Heart" have something in common? They both share the same five letters. Not just that, if you move the letter "H" from the end of "EART/**H**" to the front, it transforms into "**H**/EART." Now, call me crazy, but I don't believe this is just some random occurrence. It implies a possible connection between the Heart and the Earth, as they may share a similar nature.

When I write this, I sit in a cozy corner of our picturesque porch on the weathered wooden floor of our century-old cottage. Our timeless summer retreat stands atop Ontario's ancient bedrock, nestled at the very edge of a serene lake.

A pine tree stands between the porch's fine mesh window screens and the lake's shore. From my vantage point, the window frames form a perfect border for the picturesque arrangement of branches and twigs against the backdrop of the glimmering lake beneath the afternoon sun.

As I absorb this beautiful composition, my gaze extends to the background, beyond the pine tree's intricate details, and embraces the boundless space between the lake, the sky, and the sprawling land. It suddenly dawns on me: the space in front of me is infinite.

This vast space extends so far that it encompasses the place where my mother, brother, and sisters live on the opposite side of the globe. Although it may seem like we live in a separate world, divided by geographic distance, in reality, we coexist within the same space.

While I grasp that we all reside on the surface of the same globe, internalizing it is a different experience. It kindles within me a sense of awe and connectedness. In this moment of newfound awareness, my senses expand to include the living beings in my immediate surroundings.

The birch, spruce, and pine trees dance with the humble blueberry bush, while the chirp of birds mingles with the playful chatter of chipmunks among the rocks; even the flies resting on the window screens add a bit of charm. Together, they demonstrate how diverse nature can be.

My imagination ventures below the Earth's surface, where unseen creatures thrive. It brings to mind an article by George Monbiot, an environmental activist, who marvels at the wonders of a lump of soil when observed through a powerful lens. He shares:

> I could scarcely believe what I was seeing . . . I immediately saw springtails—tiny, animal-like insects—in dozens of shapes and sizes. Round, crabby mites were everywhere: in some soils there are half a million in every square meter . . . Roughly 90% of the species to which they belong have yet to be named. One gram of this soil—less than a teaspoonful—contains around a kilometer of fungal filaments.

How remarkable!

The Earth, with its boundless generosity, provides a home for all living beings—trees, birds, insects, fish, humans, and even unseen creatures. It imposes no restrictions, offering a haven where every entity can coexist and flourish naturally.

Without judgment, the Earth embraces and sustains each entity within its vast embrace, supporting them under the unyielding law of balance. Remarkably, this includes us, humans, despite our selfishness and destructive tendencies.

The Earth keeps its balance, even with all the different energies it deals with. Its endurance, spaciousness, and generosity stem from its ability to transmute one entity into another. Nothing is wasted; everything undergoes recycling and repurposing, with diverse life forms playing crucial roles in this process.

Just as our planet receives and transforms all that crosses its path, so too does the human heart possess the capacity to receive, absorb, and transmute the experiences and emotions it encounters. The heart is, in essence, an organ of alchemy. It bears witness and creates space for the ever-evolving nature of thoughts, emotions, energy, sensations, and perceptions, enabling them to shift, evolve, and reemerge in a new form.

At its core, the Heart Space is a gentle holding space where all feelings, thoughts, and sensations are welcome. It's a space where we can have a loving relationship with our complexity and contradiction—no pushing or pulling, just *is*. With this deliberate gentle holding, a different kind of intelligence and clarity emerges. Through this experience, we finally understand from the core of our being—in the relationship with ourselves, others, and the planet—that we are enough, whole, and always interconnected.

Within the Heart Space, our scattered thoughts and feelings can come together in a peaceful way. In this state of wholeness, our confusion and intricacies transform into beautiful simplicity. Thomas Hübl, the pioneer of collective trauma healing, beautifully expresses this sentiment, "I can rest in life only when complexity has a big enough cup to become simple."

THE POWER OF RADICAL RECEPTIVITY

Receiving gifts that come from our challenges and discomfort requires an open heart—a practice I call Radical Receptivity. This doesn't mean giving up our boundaries or saying yes to everything. No, it means learning to let go of our judgments and liberate ourselves from the grip of our preconceived notions. Judgment, in essence, is a refusal to see beyond what we think we know. We tend to shape our conception of truth based on our beliefs—a collection of repeated thoughts that provide us with a sense of certainty and familiarity. When we realize our beliefs can hold us back, we start to see the world in new ways.

Radical Receptivity grants us access to a range of subtle human faculties, accessible only when we let go of the habit of quickly jumping to conclusions. Kabir Helminski refers to these collective faculties as the "heart." He writes in *Living Presence*:

> We have subtle subconscious faculties we are not using. Beyond the limited analytical intellect is a vast realm of mind that includes psychic and extrasensory abilities; intuition; wisdom; a sense of unity; aesthetic, qualitative, and creative faculties; and image-forming and symbolic capacities. Though these faculties are many, we give them a single name with some justification, because they are operating best when they are in concert. They comprise an intelligence that is in spontaneous connection with the Universal Intelligence. This total mind we call "heart."

Understanding that the heart is a source of intelligence helps us see why Radical Receptivity matters. To receive, we need to be here, in the moment. Radical Receptivity allows us to observe and discover how our experiences shape, transform, and expand who we are. It guides us to pay attention to our inner world, showing what feels true and real to us in each moment. Through this practice, we gain a deeper understanding of ourselves and make room for our dormant, subtle abilities to offer us valuable wisdom and clear guidance in life.

However, our culture has trained us to habitually direct our attention and mental focus outward. The external world presents countless opportunities to divert our attention. We often find ourselves fixated on judging, predicting, and attempting to control their impact on us. Meanwhile, we remain unaware of the active inner world within us.

For example, picture yourself driving up to an intersection. Suddenly, the driver in front of you stops at the green light, causing you to miss your turn. In that moment, your initial reaction might involve thoughts like, "What an idiot!" or "Why is this happening to me?" These thoughts add to your growing frustration, as you dwell on cursing the other driver or perceive yourself as a victim. However, if your focus remains solely on the external situation, you may overlook the internal processes: your perception, inner dialogue, bodily sensations, and emotions that operate beyond conscious awareness.

Radical Receptivity during this driving incident invites you to tune into your inner world. This entails being receptive to what unfolds—the undeniable presence of anger. Notice the anger swirling in your chest and the intricate narrative and judgments forming in your mind. As you observe what happens inside your inner terrain, you might realize that the inattentive driver who blocked your path is not the true source of your anger. Instead, you would recognize that your anger arises from the meaning you attach to the driver's actions. This deeper insight enables you to detach from your immediate emotional response and gain a more objective understanding of the situation. It shifts your attention from blaming external circumstances to a deeper exploration of the internal dynamics that shape your experience.

Recognizing your role in creating your experience gives you the power to make a choice. You can choose to feed your rage or let wisdom guide you toward acceptance. This deliberate intention, when embraced, reveals something magical: Your thoughts will align with the changing energy of your heart.

Change your heart, and your mind will follow. Your mind will readily generate thoughts that match your new perspective. As a result, your capacity to respond beyond your conditioning will increase.

You may wonder how Radical Receptivity can be applied to difficult and complex situations. How can it be practiced when the circumstances are too painful or require someone else to change first? These questions resonated with a participant in my course who faced a challenging situation in her own life.

She shared her experience of being physically attacked by her daughter, who was grappling with mental and emotional challenges. Though they hadn't seen each other for two years, she struggled to navigate this painful dynamic. She expressed genuine fear and described her efforts of protecting herself. While she understood the concept of Radical Receptivity and its potential benefits, she feared that embracing it would leave her vulnerable to further harm. She asked me for advice on how to approach this complex situation.

Imagine having a ball covered in prickly thorns in your palm. It's a part of you, yet it inflicts great pain. Some people may attempt to remove it by throwing it away, thinking, "Why keep something that causes pain?" Yet, getting rid of it would mean losing a piece of yourself. Others may choose to fight it, clutching it even tighter, only to find the pain spreading through their entire bodies, making it impossible for them to move with their lives.

What would you do with it? How do you handle this thorny ball?

If you approach it with Radical Receptivity, you would gently hold the ball in your palm, with care. In doing so, you can still sense its presence, but it doesn't hurt you as much. Over time, you'll discover that you can move through life freely despite its existence.

This thorny ball represents suffering, which can manifest in various forms, such as past relationships, negative emotions, depression, anxiety, anger, physical pain, chronic diseases, trauma, or, in the case of the woman in my course, a painful relationship with her daughter.

Radical Receptivity creates space for introspection, allowing her to access the depth of her Heart Space. By gently holding space for her pain rather than resisting it or letting fear dominate her mind, she can recognize the profound love she has for her daughter. This revelation brings to light the tireless efforts and genuine intentions she has dedicated over the years—often overlooked and underappreciated. Simultaneously, she can allow herself to acknowledge her fear and the need for self-protection while mourning her strained relationship. Embracing the full spectrum of her emotions and exploring her inner world becomes a path to healing. Through this process, she finds the strength to navigate the challenges in her relationship and develops a greater capacity to accept what's beyond her control.

When you see the big picture, compassion, understanding, and wisdom emerge to guide you in each moment. The thorns you carry can give you greater self-awareness and allow you to move gently while remaining connected with everything. You can be with your discomfort without having to suffer from it. Furthermore, as you learn to relax into the present moment, it becomes easier to hold the anxiety and fear at bay. When you approach life with an open heart, even darkness and uncertainty can be seen clearly, and from that place of newfound clarity, you have the power to transform them into sources of light.

Fear and worry shouldn't be conquered; rather, they should be embraced with tender, loving care, like a child needing a hug. Before you try to solve your anxiety and fear, try simply being with them, not as someone under their power, but as someone older, wiser, and more loving. Embrace them as you would embrace a child and tell them, "I understand. I see you. You are part of me. I will not judge you." Take a moment in silence with your feelings. As you recognize these feelings for what they are, they begin to calm and release their grip on you.

Through the Heart Space, you'll learn a different kind of knowing that isn't always easy for the human mind to understand. Even if you don't fully grasp it, you can gain insight by sensing and feeling it. Embracing this process requires humility. After all, humility is a different face of wisdom. The incredible part is that it happens inside you, with only your awareness as a necessary ingredient. You must be present to witness the transmutation, for you are the heart of it all. The world is not "out there" where you watch and analyze from a distance; the world is happening within you, as the ancient saying goes: "As within so without, as above so below."

Everything you encounter mirrors the shifts happening within, for what you perceive is what you receive in return.

THE ART OF NOT KNOWING

A young scholar came to visit Ma, the great old turtle. He pointed at a soaring tree right next to him. He asked her, "If nothing is fixed and everything is possible, can this red pine tree become a different kind of tree?"

Ma looked at the young man, pressed her long claws into the ground, and slowly picked up some dirt.

Showing the dirt to the young man, she asked, "What is this?"

"It's dirt," he replied.

The great old turtle put the dirt back on the ground and pointed to a tree beside her. She asked, "What about that?"

"That is an oak," answered the man.

Then, suddenly, a little animal darted out of one tree and leaped to seek refuge in another nearby. "What exactly would you call that?" Ma inquired as their eyes followed the animal's movement.

"Obviously, it's a squirrel," the man replied.

Looking back at him, she said, "The dirt, the oak, the squirrel, the grass, the insects, and other forest creatures are the red pine tree that is right next to you."

"What do you mean?" The young scholar seemed confused.

"When pine needles fall to the ground, decay, and give the ground vital nutrients, humans call them soil. When the vital nutrients that come from the pine needles on the ground are digested and moved to the other trees and plants nearby, humans call them an oak, a birch, a spruce, grass, or even a red pine. When the cones are eaten by the hungry animals and give them the energy to live, humans call them squirrels, woodpeckers, and other forest creatures. And when the seeds fall, buried in the ground, and grow into a new tree, humans call them a young red pine tree." She answered him.

As the young man watched a few dried pine needles fall away from their mother tree, Ma paused for a moment to allow the seed of insight to land on the soil of the young scholar's heart.

She took a deep breath and continued, "The Pine, Oak, Squirrel, Soil, Cloud, Air, Lake, and anything that can be named in the human mind are a series of flows and fluid relationships that hold together long enough to be considered a 'thing'; until they become something else."

"In my world," Ma continued, "they are all called by one name: Life. Life, with its evolving form of possibilities, is beyond what the human mind can comprehend."

Sighing, she said, "Humans cannot see possibilities because they have different names for everything they see, hear, feel, touch, and taste. The power you were given to name things has made your finite mind believe that a *red pine* is just a red pine, a *cloud* is just a cloud, an *apple* is just an apple, and the *earth* is just the earth."

"We must be willing to see it all the way through to discover the possibilities that exist right under our noses."

Our clear-cut definitions of the world have deafened us, preventing us from seeing the dynamic flow and interconnection of our reality. Though it seems helpful, carrying these definitions is burdensome and creates tension and rigidity. Alternatively, when you're curious, you become less defensive about what emerges in each moment, and by dismantling the precise definitions we've held in our finite minds, we open a gateway to a whole fresh new way of experiencing reality.

As you learn to reduce the complexity of your own mind, you can release your grip on things beyond your control. You can even entertain the crazy idea of trusting the unknown with an unwavering conviction that you are being guided in all circumstances. Letting go of who your survival mind believes you are brings about a remarkable shift. You increasingly immerse yourself in the divine flow of life, filled with joy and contentment without apparent reason; for the mind that no longer resists is no longer in fear.

In many ways, life is a lot like the ocean—deep, vast, and full of mystery. And just like the ocean, there is always more to explore and discover. Our minds are like boats floating on the surface of this great big thing called life, and sometimes, it can feel like we're all alone out here. But the good news is that we don't have to know everything! In fact, it's better that we don't, because when we're open to not knowing, life starts to surprise us with its magic.

As John O'Donohue's poem goes:

> I would love to live
> like a river flows,
> carried by the surprise
> of its own unfolding.

So many events occur that are beyond our ability to comprehend. Things that we do not always understand are here to support us twenty-four hours a day, seven days a week.

> Your heart is beating;
> you don't have to think about it.

Your immune system repairs itself;
you don't have to project-manage it.

The trees are growing;
you don't have to plan it.

The sun rises every morning;
you don't have to work on it.

As you come to recognize that the power and intelligence of all these things are the same power and intelligence that work in you, your sense of separation from life fades away.

As you see more from your heart, you learn that life is not just one thing or the other. You can welcome a wide spectrum of experiences. You can live in peace with your survival mind, knowing the good intention in its design. All it wants is to protect you from harm and to keep you alive.

When you live from your Heart Space, your life is no longer about attaining, achieving, optimizing, fixing, or making something better—it's not even about transcending your "lower" self to a "higher" self. None of these! The Heart Space releases you from the need to engage in such pursuits. When you cultivate a loving relationship with all your glorious complexity, there is nothing left to fix. Instead, you will return to harmony as a unified whole.

No matter what our minds see on the outside, our hearts let us see the unchanging inner truth—that, beyond our worries, we are well, whole, and always being guided whether we are aware of it or not. In that trust, we can sense and feel the direction that pulls us the most. There is no right or wrong, just what feels right. No matter what we do next, it will be good for what it is, and whatever happens, it's meant for our learning.

We are not broken. We unintentionally create so many cuts in our thinking that we end up working against ourselves. The thoughts that appear in your mind do not require fixing; they only require understanding.

The path of the heart is not about controlling or changing your mind. It is about cultivating a willingness to let go of false identification and returning to the simplicity and humility of empty-headedness and not knowing.

It's crazy how much simpler and lighter life becomes once we realize we don't have to know everything. Without the constant pressure to get things "right" and "perfect," we can relax into who we are and act without second-guessing whether we're making the right move or not.

EVERYTHING IN LIFE IS AN INVITATION

It was a gloomy, chilly, and gray autumn day. Two days of non-stop rain had hidden the sun. Days like this left me feeling helpless, and as I looked out the window, I dreaded the fact that the days would grow even shorter and darker.

During my meditation that day, a question arose: What invitation does this gloomy day provide? As I slowly opened my eyes, I gazed through the window. The autumn leaves of the trees were rustling and blowing in the wind. They looked like colorful snowflakes dancing in the air as they fell gently to the ground. Near the end of their lives, the leaves showed their true color—vibrant, unapologetic, and courageous. For the leaves, the end is not dark and gloomy but full of hope, a celebration of life. As if they know the end is a new beginning.

I felt a sense of acceptance and peace, and the answer came to me: I am invited to be one with nature, to experience it as it is now, for all the plants and trees are getting ready for winter and letting go of their leaves with total acceptance.

In my intuitive mind, I saw myself becoming one with the changing season. Then a bigger invitation arose. In the dark, cold, dreary day, can I see the Light that my soul always sees? The hope, faith, and love that never change even when it is dark outside?

"Yes, I can," I whispered. The day was still dull gray, and the sun was nowhere to be seen, but the heaviness had lifted inside me.

Every unsettling emotion and experience you encounter comes with a gift and invitation. Stress invites you to be still. Worry and anxiety encourage you to trust. Burnout implores you to rest. When overwhelmed, you're nudged to slow down. Anger opens the door to peace. Even hate calls for love.

Through Radical Receptivity, you allow your mind to be so clear that the answer will reveal itself. And it's okay if you haven't heard anything yet. Trust that the answer will unfold as you attend and attune to Life—not just the little life, but the big, encompassing Life that you are. By expanding your way of seeing, you get to know that you always have the power to move mountains.

Perhaps you can ponder what the beloved Nobel laureate in literature, Toni Morrison, said in an interview with *O Magazine* about facing the unknown when doing her work:

It's that being open—not scratching for it, not digging for it, not constructing something but being open to the situation and trusting that what you don't know will be available to you. It is bigger than your overt consciousness or your intelligence or even your gifts; it is out there somewhere, and you must let it in.

From this place, it is easy to let go and experience a profound sense of contentment and well-being. Life becomes effortless and joyful with an absolute knowing that you are being guided.

When living from your Heart Space, you can face your fears and see them for what they are. In a way, your journey with fear might be like the river described in Khalil Gibran's exquisite poem:

It is said that before entering the sea,
a river trembles with fear.

She looks back at the path she has traveled,
from the peaks of the mountains,
the long winding road crossing forests and villages.

And in front of her,
she sees an ocean so vast,
that to enter there seems nothing more than to disappear forever.
But there is no other way.

The river cannot go back.
Nobody can go back.

To go back is impossible in existence.

The river needs to take the risk of entering the ocean
because only then will fear disappear,
because that's where the river will know
it's not about disappearing into the ocean,
but of becoming the ocean.

The heart is what allows you to be fully alive and fully human. As you embrace this truth, the barriers between yourselves and others begin to crumble, revealing the inherent beauty that resides in every person, regardless of their circumstances. As you tear down the walls of separation, you open yourselves up to a richer and more fulfilling life experience. You can't hate people, yourself, or your circumstances from this place; you can only understand. As a coach and facilitator, I often witness and encounter the truth articulated by Richard Rohr, "The most redemptive thing one can do for one another is just to understand."

With heartfelt understanding, you will realize there is only love. And as you dig deeper, you allow the light of understanding to illuminate your ways of being, so that you can receive the wisdom that comes with a different kind of knowing. As Thich Nhat Hanh said in his simple yet profound words, "The more you understand, the more you love; the more you love, the more you understand. They are two sides of one reality. The mind of love and the mind of understanding are the same." The more you understand, the more you are open to receiving. The more you open to receive, the more you experience wholeness.

At the end of my "Head to Heart Mastery Course," I had

participants write reflections about what it meant to live from the Heart Space. I want to share one of those reflections with you:

> Bring love to whatever is asking for your attention in any moment. You are safe. You are seen. The Universe wants for you what you want for yourself. The way to receive it is to be open and love whatever it is. Be it neediness, jealousy, anger, judgment, love it. Bring the acceptance and understanding that it needs, wants, and deserves. Don't push away or try to change. Listen. Once you've been heard by yourself, you can listen to others. Trust the process. Trust it all.

In this ever-changing world, where familiar structures crumble, we are invited to trust the unchanging essence within ourselves while being kind and gentle with our imperfections and evolving nature. Accepting both our light and shadows allows love to find fulfillment through the act of self-witnessing. After all, only when we start witnessing can we truly see. And when we truly see, we can begin to love fully.

Love breaks the chains of fear, granting us the freedom to explore limitless possibilities. To comprehend this, we must begin with Radical Receptivity, welcoming life with an open heart and mind.

REFLECTION AT YOUR OWN PACE

1. Contemplate holding your suffering gently, like having a thorny ball in your palm. How does Radical Receptivity allow you to move with your pain and discomfort without being overwhelmed by them?
2. Explore the relationship between Radical Receptivity and listening. How does being receptive allow you to observe and inquire into your own experience? How does it shape your perception of yourself and the world around you? Reflect on a time when you were truly receptive and attentive to your inner terrain while receiving external stimulation. What did you discover about yourself?
3. Consider a situation where you consciously chose love as your guiding force. How did it differ from acting out of fear? How did it bring a sense of freedom and fulfillment? Reflect on the impact it had on your overall well-being and the choices you made.

TEN
LIVING A LIFE OF PRACTICE

> Practice, in every sense of the word, is not about reaching "doneness"; it's about staying loose and doing it again. The analogy to exercise is total: if you regularly swim or run or do meditative breathing, there is no moment when you "finish" getting fit and no longer need effort to sustain it. Nor is there any way to elevate your ability without continuous practice.
>
> ERIC LIU AND SCOTT-NOPPE BRANDON

Being in the Heart Space is a practice, as it is a practice to be kind, loving, compassionate, and to hold our contradictions gently. In practice, our muscles and understanding expand because practice makes what we do real to us. Otherwise, it is just a concept and abstraction in our mind, distant and disconnected from our felt experience. When we practice, we allow our body, mind, and heart to grow in understanding. Practice is also a means of maintaining a connection with something you want to embody and bring into reality.

In my spare time, I practice Odissi, an East Indian Classical dance form, which brings to my attention two distinct qualities of time: the performance and the rehearsal.

In performance mode, in front of an audience, you can't go back and change what you've done. You must keep going and doing your best until your dance ends. In this mode, time moves quickly, like an arrow released from a bow. Therefore, you see time as a non-renewable resource. You only get one shot at it.

In practice or rehearsal mode, time works differently, serving as a container for exploration. You can repeat, redo, refine, slow down, change directions as you move, and perfect your piece. In the life of practice, time becomes a renewable resource, affording us the opportunity to repeat, improve, and even pause. Through this process, we gain a deeper understanding of ourselves and our practice. We can respond to what we need instead of what we "think" we need.

When our minds are conditioned to believe that the *result* is all that matters, we see most aspects of our lives as a final performance. You either win or lose, succeed or fail. It's as if every decision we make is final.

No wonder we become doubtful, stressed, and constantly worry about making the right decision. But when we approach life as a practice, it becomes less daunting. We can show up each day without worrying about making a wrong turn.

Practice enables us to grasp the true significance of grace in our day-to-day lives. Instead of perceiving grace solely as a religious concept or a mental abstraction, we can recognize that divine mercy—freely given, with no strings attached—is already present and interwoven into the fabric of life. The clues are all over nature, in the constant cycle of endings and beginnings, from the changing seasons to the continual cycle of day and night. Divine grace is inherent in our ability to let go and start anew. If you choose, you can always reset and restart anytime.

Every breath is a chance to start over. Every moment is an opportunity to forgive and change our perspective. Through a life of practice, we naturally gain access to grace. Even death is grace in action.

And if grace could speak, it would say something like this:

Every moment is arriving present,
for Present is a gift of life.

The secret of time is hidden away from
the blinds, until they are willing to
open their eyes and accept the gift.

In every moment you die and are reborn.
Repeatedly without failing.

So that you can start fresh,
free from the bondage of old stories.

Walk without burden on your shoulders.
Experience every moment like the first time,
as there is no other time than now.

Why rush? This is the only life you have.
Here. Now.

The time to be deeply and powerfully alive is always now.

THE PRACTICE OF OPENING YOUR HEART

Many excellent practices are available to help you become grounded in the Heart Space, such as the Loving-Kindness meditation, which originated in the Buddhist tradition, and Centering Prayers, which came from the Contemplative Christian tradition.

For the purpose of this book, I want to emphasize practices that will expand your sense-ability, allowing you to open your heart and perception wide enough to experience everything in a fresh new way. Through these practices, you will encounter the world through a different lens—a set of eyes that hold a deeper knowing. This deeper knowing will lead you to develop inner trust and embrace your experiences as they naturally unfold.

Our heart communicates through feelings and sensations. To truly understand this inner communication, we must permit ourselves to feel and perceive without judgment. Granting ourselves this allowance is the initial step in mastering the language of the heart, leading to a deeper connection and valuable insights into our emotions and experiences.

Developing our ability to feel and sense is essential to living an authentic life. As you've learned, we've been conditioned to ignore our feelings and emotions in favor of developing the capacity to think logically and solve problems. Nonetheless, genuine inspiration, enlightenment, and insights emerge from a life lived from the heart.

EXPLORING THE DEPTHS OF FEELING AND SENSING

In Indonesian language, the word *Rasa* refers to something that functions more closely to the heart than it does to the head. The original meaning of *Rasa* in Sanskrit is nectar, essence, or taste. For centuries, *Rasa* has been taught as art theory in India's artistic traditions. It helps artists, writers, musicians, and dancers infuse their work with emotional flavors and essences that can be deeply felt by their audience. Indonesians use the word extensively in their daily conversation. Besides using it as a noun for a flavor or a taste, such as vanilla (*Rasa* vanilla), they also use it as a verb to express one's feelings, emotions, observations, sensations, and intuitions. It is interchangeable with "I feel," "I sense," "my gut feeling tells me," "I observe," and "I taste." In other words, *Rasa* is the kind of cognitive capacity that involves sensing and feeling the internal and external stimuli one receives and the ability to identify the flavor of these experiences.

Rasa is quite distinct from simply "thinking." It has a layer of experiential and spaciousness. You take in your surroundings by feeling and sensing them, then express the view from your inner experience instead of rushing to give an intellectual definition. Without *Rasa*, we are disconnected from our feelings and the world around us. It allows us to feel each other's emotions and empathize with them. *Rasa* is what enables artists and musicians to produce works that move and touch us.

Rasa is expressed and received, much like musicians convey a flavor they experience from within through the melody, rhythm, or lyrics they create. As you listen to their music, its flavor touches you and creates a feeling that only you can experience.

Rather than clinging to the habitual narratives your mind generates, *Rasa* helps you attune to your internal landscape by becoming more aware of your feelings as tangible, sensory experiences.

For example, in a challenging business meeting where your mind tends to draw conclusions about people not valuing your hard work and placing blame on you—rather than reacting with anger and potentially saying something you may regret—your awareness can uncover different layers of *Rasa*. You may become aware of physical sensations like chest constriction, bodily tension, and shortness of breath. You might notice feeling less centered and more agitated. This moment of bridging your cognition and sensory experiences creates a space for self-observation that allows you to bring intention, attention, and inner wisdom to the situation.

When you are open to receiving *Rasa*, you also have a broader vocabulary to express yourself. As an Odissi dancer, I had to learn to embody the emotional *Rasa* of the story I told in the dance. My teacher used to say that every look has a meaning and that my whole body—torso, arms, fingers, gaze, facial expression, and breath—must be able to express the range of feelings and emotions conveyed in the story.

Expressing emotions in Odissi dance proved challenging for me. My facial expressions and gaze felt rigid, lacking the depth required to convey the intended emotions. I began to improve when I imagined a ball of feeling and intention at the center of my heart, radiating outward through my breath, the muscles of my body, and my facial expressions, all while keeping my feet grounded on the floor. From that point on, my ability to express feelings and emotions in Odissi dramatically improved.

This newfound approach to embodying emotions extends to other aspects of my life. My heart felt more open. The ability to express my emotions fully, without judgment, allowed me to direct my intentions and communicate with greater precision and authenticity. Embodying *Rasa* can strengthen how we carry and channel our intention and attention. This can be incredibly useful in both personal and professional relationships. When you can understand and articulate your emotions, you can easily find common ground and build strong connections with others.

With that in mind, I invite you to be open and observe your experience as you begin the practices below. Even if you have done similar exercises, maintain a beginner's mind. Every experience is brand new, and what didn't work for you three years ago may work for you today. Pay close attention to what arises within you. When it feels "right," consider integrating it into your daily routine. These exercises aren't just techniques to adopt; they're an invitation to encounter the extraordinary within everyday experiences, enabling you to gain understanding through direct felt-sense experience rather than mere intellectual knowing.

1. PRACTICE SLOWING DOWN: THE MOST IMPORTANT PRACTICE IN OUR HECTIC WORLD

To be aware of *Rasa*, we need to slow down. We need time and space to feel, sense, digest information, and extract meaning from our experiences. As an acclaimed travel writer, Pico Iyer, says, "The more information we have, the more space we need to make sense of it."

When you slow down, you give yourself the opportunity to access your awareness. There is no hack or secret way of doing it. Take time to slow down, and you will see your deepest thoughts, beliefs, motivations, feelings, and sensations. In doing so, the unconscious, hidden, and fleeting can be seen beneath the surface. When you are aware, you can simply ask: How does my experience at this moment touch me?

Your survival mind can only perceive results when doing something and exerting effort. However, sometimes exerting effort becomes the obstacle to getting what you want. Imagine trying hard to relax or making a significant effort to surrender; the opposite will surely occur. The same is true for slowing down. Through practice, you can let your survival mind perceive that non-doing can also yield results.

SPACIOUSNESS IS EMBEDDED IN EVERYTHING

The space between two musical notes is what allows you to hear a melody. In the same way, the space between your inhalation and exhalation completes your breathing. A break between your heartbeats enables the heart to rest and keep beating. A pause in the conversation allows a fresh new thought to emerge. When you begin to notice and appreciate these pauses, silences, and stillness in your surroundings, even if only for a brief moment, you'll gradually become attuned to the quieter, more tranquil part of your mind. This connection allows you to access a deeper knowing that exists beyond thought and words.

THE APPLICATION OF SLOWING DOWN IN EVERYDAY LIFE

You can also practice slowing down while actively engaging in a task. Start with the little things you do daily.

> Slow down your breath,
> and you'll be more aware of
> what is alive in you more than ever before.

> Slow down your walk,
> and you'll notice your footsteps
> and the distance you've traveled.

> Slow down when you eat,
> and you'll enter a daily sacred ritual
> where what grows on the ground
> nourishes and becomes part of you.

> Slow down your thinking,

and you'll begin to see the kind of reality
your thoughts are creating for you.

Slow down your speech,
and you'll weave a magical pause
that enables you to listen more deeply.

Slow down when you love someone,
and you'll be present for them
in a way that no one else ever has,
free from all expectations and judgments.

The most precious aspects of life, such as love, relationships, creativity, and intimacy, cannot be rushed. I believe the only way to see the beauty within the ordinary is by slowing down. With that in mind, I extend an invitation to use *Rasa* to cultivate a more profound and richer experience of life.

EXERCISE: TRAINING YOUR BRAIN TO NOTICE SPACE IN BETWEEN

Our brains often prioritize movement and action over stillness. To rewire this tendency, we can use our bodies and senses to help our brain embrace the pleasant sensation of slowing down.

1. Begin by setting your attention and intention to slow down, focusing on being fully present in the exercise.
2. Decide how much time you'll practice this exercise, such as 3 or 5 minutes, or even more if you're

comfortable. Setting a specific timeframe helps you stay committed and fully engaged in the experience.
3. Focus on your breath and feel the rhythm of your inhales and exhales. Let this simple act of focusing on your breath anchor you to the present moment.
4. As you become more grounded with your breathing, gently shift your attention to the pauses and spaces between different elements in your body or your surroundings. For example, the pause between someone's words, between your inhalation and exhalation, the gap from one sound to another, from one heartbeat to another, the space between objects in front of you, or the silence between raindrops.
5. Spend some time with one stimulus before shifting your attention. Use your senses to notice the length and quality of the pause. Stay open and curious as you observe the sensations in your body. Do you notice any differences in your experience? Is there a rhythm to it? Pay attention to the pause, empty spaces, and silence in between; observe how this impacts the quality of your attention. How does it make you feel? If you find it enjoyable, savor the experience. Rather than quickly moving your attention elsewhere, create space for your heart, mind, and body to fully embrace these feelings and sensations.
6. If your mind wanders or distractions arise, gently bring your focus back to your breath and the

spaces you observe. Be patient with yourself and approach the practice with a non-judgmental attitude.
7. Embrace these brief pauses as opportunities to slow down and find tranquility amidst life's constant motion. Be fully present and attuned to these subtleties, savoring the peacefulness they bring.

With regular practice, you may find it easier to recall this sense of calm and spaciousness throughout your day. Let this newfound awareness of "space" enrich your experiences and interactions, cultivating a greater sense of presence and mindfulness in your life.

2. PRACTICE TO LISTEN

When we take a moment to pause and listen, something incredible happens. We become aware of the details that often go unnoticed. Our minds no longer need to work hard to produce various thoughts or opinions about what we hear. This allows us to simply receive what is presented to us. Listening can be a powerful tool that enables us to connect with ourselves, our loved ones, and our environment.

THE APPLICATION OF LISTENING IN EVERYDAY LIFE

The first time I tried this simple exercise, I was surprised by the ease of listening. Listening without thinking or judging made me hear things more clearly than ever before. This experience taught me the true meaning of *ease* because I felt much lighter, and my body relaxed when I let go of the need to form opinions about everything I heard.

Listening heals our separation. When we listen with an open heart, we allow ourselves to have a deeper connection and greater understanding of what we're listening to, whether that's the nature around us, our body, our feelings, or another person's longing and desire.

Perhaps we can listen to Wiruungga Dunggiirr, a First Nations Australian Elder, on the importance of listening, "If you don't listen, you'll never learn. You won't go through the changes if you don't listen. Listen to your heart and what you're feeling inside. If you don't take notice, it's going to make you sick." As an elder, he encourages his people to sleep with a leaf or near a tree, listening to the heartbeat of the tree, the flowing water, and even practicing deep meditation to attune to these natural sounds. He explains that through deep listening, one can connect more deeply with one's spirit and the elements—water, wind, and more—because everything is interconnected through listening.

I have been facilitating deep listening group practices for the last few years and have witnessed how this practice cultivates open hearts by creating a space within yourselves and with others. When you transition from speaking "about" to speaking "from," you form deeper connections filled with mutual respect, relatedness, insight, and wisdom. Through this kind of presence and attentive listening, you can experience what it's like to be truly seen.

The best gift we can give others and ourselves is the

opportunity to be received just as we are. This means listening to someone not based on what matters to you, but on what matters to them. You listen not according to your expectations but to who they truly are. Nor do you listen with judgment; instead, you openly accept what is alive in them.

When you're open to listening and receiving, you can also ask yourselves deeper and more honest questions.

When I am having a conversation with you:

- Am I so occupied in my mind that I only see what I want to see?
- Can I genuinely feel what you feel?
- Can I accept you as you are instead of trying to be right or fix you?

When I am alone:

- Can I free myself from my own expectations and be imperfectly human?
- Can I honor myself as a human with strengths and weaknesses?
- Can I let myself be me and be seen?

When I connect with my children:

- Am I trusting them enough to let them make mistakes while also supporting them unconditionally?
- Am I trying to fit them into my expectations and seeing only what I want to see?

- Am I nurturing them with love or with fear?
- Am I making my opinion the most important thing?
- Can I be quiet while holding them lovingly in my arms, understanding my presence means more than my words?

When you listen, you can tune into your inner experience and better understand your wants, needs, and perspectives. Only then can you respond with clarity, compassion, and understanding.

EXERCISE: LISTENING AS THE PRACTICE OF RECEIVING

For this exercise, I invite you to listen to your surroundings as if you are receiving what you are paying attention to. Take it in without analyzing or exerting effort. Experience the difference between receiving and having to figure things out or needing to analyze what you see or hear. Just receive.

1. Choose a dedicated time for this exercise. It could be 3 minutes, 5 minutes, or 15 minutes—whatever feels suitable to you. You can also do this in between your business meetings or while taking a short break in between your activities.
2. Find a comfortable place to sit down, close your eyes, and begin by focusing on your breath. Allow yourself to feel grounded in the present moment.
3. Gently open your eyes and shift your focus to your sense of sight. Instead of actively seeking out

specific objects to look at, allow objects to come into your view naturally. Let your gaze wander, and when it settles on an object, receive its textures, colors, and shape as if you are welcoming them into your eyes. Let gentle curiosity accompany your attention. Enjoy the experience of simply receiving what you see without the need to analyze or interpret.
4. As you practice, try to discern the difference between "focusing" on the objects and "allowing" the objects to come to your awareness. Pay attention to the quality of your sight and observe how it makes you feel. Notice the sense of effortlessness that comes with simply allowing objects to come to you as they are.
5. After 2-4 minutes of visual receptivity, gently close your eyes and shift your focus to your sense of hearing. Listen closely to the sounds around you. Receive each sound as it reaches your ears. Observe its quality and direction. Do you perceive the subtle differences in your experience between this form of receiving sounds and regular listening? Notice how these sounds touch you and resonate within your body.

If you find joy in this practice, feel free to extend the duration of the auditory reception.

Regularly engaging in this exercise will allow you to access your Heart Space and receive the world around you without judgment. As you do so, your body learns a new way of being—one without resistance—and it will begin to relax. Simultaneously, your mind liberates itself from the burden of constant overthinking and figuring things out. It will come to realize that simply being present and receptive is enough.

3. PRACTICE TO NOTICE GOOD FEELINGS WITHIN

To experience genuine happiness and pleasure, I invite you to look inward, recognizing that good feelings originate from within. While external events can bring temporary happiness, there is a wellspring of bliss that comes from simply being ourselves.

Throughout life, we develop habitual ways of facing the world, encoded unconsciously in our muscle tensions, posture, and breathing patterns. For me, feeling powerless and anxious had become so familiar that my subconscious reaction to most challenges was, "I have no control." Others may face the world with a strong "nobody likes me" or "I do not matter." These deeply ingrained, pervasive beliefs shape our thought patterns day after day, even when circumstances change. As a result, our emotional range becomes restricted, hindering our ability to experience genuine happiness, joy, serenity, and relaxation. Can you relate to this experience?

To break free from a restricted emotional range, a simple yet powerful practice involves becoming more aware of positive sensations and emotions within your body. Often, our minds overlook these pleasant feelings, as they are preoccupied with focusing on problems. But if you deliberately pay attention to when you feel good, you'll notice that these feelings happen more often than you realize. Knowing they are always within your reach can give you a sense of ease.

THE APPLICATION OF NOTICING GOOD FEELINGS IN EVERYDAY LIFE

Our default way of thinking can make us feel stuck and focus solely on our pain and suffering. We should rekindle our childlike sense of wonder and learn to rediscover the joy in simple, ordinary moments to break free from this mental trap.

Picture yourself watching an exciting movie in your comfy living room, completely captivated by the storyline. And consider this: Just because you're lost in the movie doesn't mean the couch you're sitting on disappears, does it? In the same way, when we're immersed in unpleasant emotions, we may overlook the calm and secure feelings within us. These feelings are waiting to be accessed when we direct our attention toward them.

In tough times, when we experience pain, tension, fear, doubt, stress, anxiety, or despair, we can tap into our reservoir of spaciousness, connection, grace, clarity, strength, pleasure, joy, peace, and trust. By realizing that we can access good feelings even in difficult times, we can find comfort in knowing that external circumstances cannot take away our innate well-being.

Let's begin with a simple exercise to help your body notice more pleasant sensations, without being overly influenced by thoughts or mental chatter.

EXERCISE: NOTICING GOOD FEELINGS

1. Pick a simple activity that allows you to slow down, such as drinking tea, taking a leisurely walk in the park, sitting quietly, meditating, or doing gentle movement exercises. Choose a comfortable length of time for the practice: 3, 5, or 10 minutes.
2. Set your attention and intention to be fully present in the chosen activity.
3. Begin by focusing on your breath to ground yourself in the present moment.
4. As you center yourself, tune in to your body and be mindful of any subtle, pleasant sensations or feelings of well-being that arise. Take the time to explore these feelings with curiosity and an open heart. For instance, if you are drinking tea, bring your attention to the pleasure of smelling the aroma as you get the cup to your lips, or savor the warmth of the cup in your palms. If you are walking in the park, notice the joy of gliding your arms leisurely or feel the gentle caress of the wind on your face. Whatever the activity may be, allow yourself to be fully present and find pleasure in these simple moments, even if it's just for a brief moment.
5. Allow your attention to flow from one enjoyable sensation to the next. There's no need to analyze or measure these feelings; doing so will take you away from them. Simply experience them in whatever form they reveal themselves to you.

Good feelings don't depend on future events or circumstances. They are experiences that unfold moment by moment. To truly feel them, you need to be "here" and receptive to them

4. PRACTICE SURRENDERING

Surrendering isn't the result of our actions; instead, it's a product of our understanding and awareness. When we surrender, we let go of our firm grip on how things should unfold and trust that whatever happens will ultimately be for the best, even when we don't yet fully comprehend it. This demands courage and a deep understanding of who we truly are and how reality works.

Surrendering can be intimidating, yet it is remarkably liberating and empowering. It's an act fueled by faith, trust, and love. Surrendering means letting go of personal agendas and being open to possibilities. This act grants us the freedom to be present, unburdened by the need to constantly strive or fight for control.

Surrender is relational. To surrender, I must trust something else, which, in turn, transforms both me and what I trust into *us*. You must be willing to let go of control and place faith in another, whether that be a person, a thing, or God. Trust empowers us to rely on the strength of the connection to guide us. Instead of responding in isolation, you are informed by the unfolding relationship between yourself and what you are surrendering to. Deliberate surrender cannot happen without trust.

I have come to understand that surrender works like exercising our muscles. Just as a gymnast can't twist and bend without muscle training, surrender involves conditioning our natural survival instincts. These instincts are responsible for our body's concerns about safety. For instance, imagine if I were to ask you to fall backward without any support or assurance of safety, your body's natural reaction would be to resist, and you wouldn't be willing to do it. However, if you have thick cushions or other supportive elements in place, and you check and confirm it's safe, your body will be more willing to follow your command to fall backward. Through regular practice and starting small, we can train our nervous system to understand that it's okay to let go and surrender.

My understanding of trust and surrender grew from one mundane experience. One day, I was on my way to catch the subway train for an important business meeting. My home is just a five-minute walk from the station, so the trip should've been easy. However, the fear of missing the train and the importance of the meeting consumed me. Racing against time, I walked as fast as I could. My body tensed up, and my breaths became shorter and shallower with every step. Those 5 minutes felt like an eternity. All I could think about was not being late.

Fortunately, I reached the station before the train arrived. It was in that moment of relief a realization struck me: I could have stayed calm by simply noticing that my feet were doing their job in getting me to the station. No wonder my mind felt anxious. When it was preoccupied, it failed to recognize its connection to my body. It wasn't even aware I had legs, and those legs were walking as fast as they could!

This insight showed me that I could place my trust not only in the significant aspects of life but also in the smallest ones: in my hands to perform tasks, my feet to carry me, my mind to generate ideas, and my body to heal. Noticing the intelligence at work within my body opens my eyes to the intelligence that governs all things beyond my comprehension.

By cultivating trust and surrender in the minutiae of life, I discovered the power of surrendering to something greater than myself. This was not a blind act. Instead, it came from a deep and personal understanding that surrendering to something greater could connect me to a powerful source of wisdom and guidance that had previously seemed distant and hard to reach.

THE APPLICATION OF SURRENDERING IN EVERYDAY LIFE

Surrendering cannot be forced. It must come from one's willingness.

We're conditioned to believe that things won't happen unless we make them happen. However, surrendering can show us that life can and does unfold *for* us and *through* us, even when we're not actively striving for it. When we choose to surrender, the constant chatter of our minds fades away, and we become aware of the subtle movements and serendipitous moments in our lives.

We can appreciate and understand that life co-creates with us by witnessing the unfolding movements of surrender. We never work alone; we work with the interconnected web of life that supports us. With this awareness, we can release our burdens, relinquish control, and place more trust in life.

For trust is like your feet.

When you trust,
you take one step toward what you want.

Come to Life with trust.
When you question yourself, you question Life.

To live, you don't have to do much.
To live means you are supported by many things from inside and outside.

You don't have to create the air you breathe.
You even don't need to try hard to breathe;
your body does it for you.

The 30 trillion cells of your body and 39 trillion friendly microbiome cells living in you are alive.
As they are doing their own things together,
they are supporting you.

When you trust, you begin to feel light.
In the light and lightness, you are free and fluid.

In simplicity of your being,
you move and receive.

As you practice surrendering, these questions offer valuable points for reflection:

- How can I be still and know that I am held?
- How can I interact with myself and the life around me in a way that embraces trust and connection?

- What are some difficult emotions or life circumstances I can learn to accept?
- What am I holding onto that I could let go?
- What would it take for me to release my expectations and trust the process?

Here are more questions to help you explore the possibilities of letting go and surrendering:

- What space could I create if I release my attachment to being right?
- How might I grow if I embrace and welcome discomfort?
- What might be possible if I trust the unknown?
- Who could I become if I let go of my fear and anxiety?

EXERCISE: WALKING WITH YOUR EYES CLOSED

You are familiar with this exercise from Chapters 5 and 6. To begin, find a safe, familiar place like a park nearby or a room at home. Do this exercise for one to three minutes each time. You can do it a few times throughout the day.

1. Find your center. Inhale and exhale deeply. Let your mind and body enter a state of peace and mindfulness.
2. Set your intention to let go. Take a moment to focus on surrendering to the experience.

3. Gently close your eyes and take a slow, deliberate step forward. As you walk, place your trust in your body, the sensations in your feet, and the solidity of the ground beneath you. If necessary, slow down and tread cautiously, focusing on each step you take. Pay special attention to the sensation of your feet touching the ground, and, most importantly, embody the meaning of surrender. This means letting go of the need for control and fully immersing yourself in the present moment, allowing the act of walking to become a meditative practice.
4. If you start to feel nervous or uneasy, don't judge or try to push it away. Instead, acknowledge and hold that feeling gently. When you sense the need to open your eyes briefly, please do so. Regain your center and then continue with your eyes closed. Repeat this process as needed.
5. As you surrender to the experience, observe how your balance and relationship with your body, senses, breath, and the surrounding environment change.
6. Take a moment for self-reflection with these questions:

- How does it feel to gently embrace the unsettling feeling of not knowing while also carrying the intention to surrender
- What do you observe when you surrender to this experience?

5. PRACTICE EMBODYING INTENTION

The root word of intention, *intendere*, comes from Latin. "In" means "towards," and "tendere" means "to stretch." Thus, intention means stretching your attention towards something.

Intention gives soul to your attention. It animates your attention and shapes your actions. When you act without conscious intention, your actions are simply a rendering of habit. Consequently, your future becomes merely a repetition of your past.

Intention requires alignment, meaning that your whole self—including your spirit, mind, and body—moves in unison. To follow through on an intention involves surrendering to a particular intent.

While it may seem contradictory, an act of surrender is, in fact, an act of commitment. Both require continuous resistance to provocations, doubts, and distractions. You must allow your intent to come alive through all of your faculties.

Just as a ship needs an anchor to prevent it from drifting away, we need intention to keep us grounded against the strong currents of distraction. Intention provides us with purpose and direction in every moment. It helps us remain focused on what truly matters, regardless of whether we are winning or losing. After all, intention can only be carried out in the present.

If we could carry our intention like we carry our mobile phone and check in with it as frequently as we check our emails and social media, we would be much more productive, focused, fulfilled, and happy. Don't you think so?

THE APPLICATION IN EVERYDAY LIFE

In our fast-paced lives that prioritize performance and productivity, it can be easy to transition from one task to the next without pausing to be intentional. We rush from one virtual call to the next and constantly multitask, often maintaining autopilot as our default mode.

While some may disagree, I believe that concentrating on intention holds more power than fixating solely on a goal. Unlike a goal, which tends to be future-focused and often feels distant and disconnected, intention operates in the present moment. It works like an archer preparing to shoot an arrow—what evolve now dictates how the arrow is released and where it lands. The present shapes the future. Intention is closer to us and more adaptable than a goal, providing direction without making us inflexible.

Deliberate intention is connected to our genuine desires and inner guidance, typically arising from a place of authenticity and fueled by a strong sense of purpose and heartfelt commitment.

Here are some questions to ask yourself:

- How do I know if my words and actions are true to my intentions?
- How does it feel to set an intention from my Heart Space?
- How can I make what I say and express reflect my intentions?
- How has my intention impacted the outcome of my activities?

- How can I stay mindful of my Heart Space and ensure my intentions are rooted in love, compassion, and authenticity?
- How can I use this practice to maintain a more consistent focus on my intentions?

EXERCISE: CARRYING YOUR INTENTION

In East Indian dance, I perform *pranam*, a gesture of respect, both before and after my dance practice. This ritual involves brief body and hand movements to honor Mother Earth, show respect to the teacher, and acknowledge the ground on which we dance.

Similarly, when my son enters or exits his karate dojo, he bows as a sign of humility and respect to the dojo, his teachers, and his peers. Hindus in Bali prepare *canang sari* offerings every morning. These offerings consist of a burned stick of incense placed in a basket woven from palm leaves filled with colorful flower petals as a gesture of devotion. Catholics kneel and make the sign of the cross before entering their pew as a sign of respect.

These diverse rituals all have something in common: intentional practice. By setting an intention, we can open ourselves up to participate fully in what we are creating. Through humble bows and meaningful gestures, the intention of respect and devotion is shared between individuals and communities alike.

In this exercise, you'll create intentional space by choosing an activity that takes 5 to 30 minutes to complete. It could be a movement meditation, enjoying a cup of tea, tidying up, or having a conversation with someone. Ensure that the activity has a clear beginning and end.

1. Set your intention: As you begin, picture yourself entering a dedicated space with your intention in mind. Pause to take a deep breath and place your hand over your heart to connect with that intention. Now, fully immerse yourself in your intentional space.
2. Whether it involves sipping tea, washing dishes, or engaging with a loved one, keep your intention close to your heart. Let it permeate your breath, actions, and words. If you find your mind wandering and forgetting your intention, gently return to it while engaged in the task.
3. As you conclude the activity, repeat the same gestures—take a moment to breathe intentionally while placing your palm over your heart. Express what you need to express in the moment. Visualize yourself exiting the intentional space.

Afterward, reflect on these questions to deepen your experience:

- How did my intention feel in my body?
- How did my activity alter in quality when I approached it with deliberate intention?
- What insights can I gather from this experience?
- How can I further develop this practice and apply this intention to other aspects of my life?

6. HEART-CENTERED PRACTICE

My body is a complex network of cells, organs, and systems, all intricately connected by an invisible force that binds them together. I often wonder how trillions of separated parts recognize that they are a member of a single organism, culminating as *me*.

The word "gravity" popped into my head as I thought of this. Just as the Earth's gravity pulls everything toward its center, our bodies seem to possess a similar gravitational force that intelligently holds each cell and awareness together, facilitating their harmonious functioning, including repair and regeneration. This binding force unites them into a single entity with a shared essence.

Now, I invite you to acknowledge the immense gravitational power emanating from your heart, shaping not just your physical well-being but also your emotions and spirit. The heart is remarkable. Scientific research reveals that the heart's magnetic field is over 100 times stronger than the brain's and can be detected up to 3 feet away from your body. It's the source of our energy and vitality, and throughout ancient times, it has been considered the very seat of our soul.

When we shift the center of our being from our head to our heart, we open ourselves up to a different kind of intelligence—one that is more universal, connected, highly compatible and adaptable with the fabric of life.

Indeed, every emotion and feeling resides in the heart. It's the heart that loves and experiences joy, compassion, happiness, as well as sadness and grief. And it's the heart that gives us the power to carry on even when we may want to give up. Our hearts not only feel but also radiate these emotions into the world. When we share our hearts with others, we create a profound and soulful connection, transmitting our feelings and intentions to them.

Shifting your center of gravity from your head to your heart can be done in many ways. Here are few exercises to try:

EXERCISE 1: BASIC BREATHING AWARENESS

Do you know what's truly amazing? When you pay full attention to your breathing, it automatically slows down, and you start to feel more relaxed.

I call this state *simplicity*—an ordinary perfection that our survival mind often overlooks. It's a state of homeostasis where there's nothing to fix, nowhere to go, and nothing to do other than breathe.

The best part is that you can tap into this feeling anytime and anywhere by giving your breath a little love and attention. All it takes is 30 seconds to 1 minute—during a meeting, your commute, a Zoom call, or even while doing chores.

Ready to try it out?

1. Find a cozy spot to sit, or if you're busy with something, set aside a specific time to give this simple breathing exercise a go.
2. To begin, set your intention to commit to this exercise for a specific duration.
3. Start by becoming aware of your breath.
4. As you become more aware, observe your moment-by-moment inhalation and exhalation. Notice how your body naturally moves and responds to it. Be with your breath without trying

to control it—there is no need to strive for perfection.
5. If your mind starts to wander (and trust me, it happens to all of us), gently bring your focus back to your breath. There is no need for judgment—just return to the present moment, as if nothing happened.
6. Allow yourself to be fully present, relishing the experience of being here, right now, with your breath and body.
7. When you feel ready, conclude your practice. Take a moment to notice if you feel any different after the exercise before moving on to your next activity.

EXERCISE 2: BEING RELATIONAL WITH YOUR BREATH

Have you ever wondered how food tastes without salt or spices? It's pretty bland, right? Well, that taste is similar to breathing without adding conscious intention. In the exercise above, we've introduced focusing attention on our breath. Now, imagine what would happen if we add deliberate intention to the mix.

It's intriguing how our breath mirrors our state of mind, consistently adapting to the subtleties of our thoughts and emotions. When worry arises, our breath responds. When experiencing anxiety, our heartbeat accelerates. Instead of exhaling, we might unknowingly hold our breath, which can intensify anxiety. Our breath becomes a flavorful indicator of our emotions.

Your breath's influence is a two-way street. It's bi-directional and capable of impacting your state of mind as well. For example, prolonged shallow breathing after hours of sitting can affect your mental state. On the other hand, directing your attention to your breath during moments of stress releases tension in your body, allowing you to feel calmer.

Do you recall the story from Chapter 8 about cymatics art and Kenichi Kanazawa's creation of geometric shapes from sand particles on a vibrating steel plate? Well, the following exercise is a simple example of how you can shift the formation of your breath by vibrating the steel plate of your being.

1. Start with Exercise 1.
2. As you become more present with your breath, meditate on this question: If your breath were a guest in your body, how would you want it to feel?
3. Allow your answer to influence your breath. Pay attention to the subtle shifts in your breathing pattern and the way you connect with your breath. It might spark an image about how you embrace your breath. You might sense spaciousness in your awareness, a rush of gratitude, a little smile, or experience a shift in certain parts of your body. Alternatively, you might find that nothing changes at all. Explore and embrace whatever unfolds.

Simply be in a relationship with your breath, and let your intention guide the kind of relationship you want to build with it. You can do this for as little as 5 minutes a day.

EXERCISE 3: RADIATING FROM THE HEART

Have you ever considered your connection to the sun?

The sun has played a central role in sustaining human existence. Ancient cultures even worshipped it as a deity. Even though we're not physically close to the sun, we can still feel its essence and influence. Those rays travel 93 million miles, and you can feel their warmth on your skin.

Now consider the sun's light. Are you aware that you can't directly see the light itself? Instead, you perceive its existence through the objects it illuminates. When you look at the radiant sky, colorful clouds, and all the surfaces it touches, you don't see the light itself, but rather the effects it produces. What enables you to see the world around you is the very element that remains invisible to you.

Your heart is the sun of your body, the center of your being. Its influence extends well beyond the confines of your skin. Without it, your actions lack depth, significance, and connection. The heart is the pulse of any relationship.

It is important to be mindful of your light source and cultivate it with your awareness. Otherwise, you waste the power you have to impact the world. You may not see the light that emanates from your heart, but its presence can be felt by others.

If you take away only one thing from this book, let it be this: The way you change the world or make an impact doesn't come from what you do, but from what your heart projects. Every thought you think and every word you say is a prayer emanating from your heart. It gives you the power to love, feel, and experience all the joy and happiness life can offer. Your heart is your essence—it's what makes you who you are. May you never take it for granted.

Practicing awareness of what you emanate from your heart can be powerful. When you recognize the energy you emit, aligning your thoughts, emotions, and beliefs with your highest intentions becomes easier. This awareness empowers you to make positive shifts and embrace a more intentional and purposeful way of being.

Spend any time between 5 to 15 minutes on this exercise.

1. Start with Exercise 1 to get yourself centered.
2. As you become more present with your breath, shift your awareness to your heart.
3. Let your breath flow in and out of your heart. Inhale love and light, and exhale any tension or resistance.
4. When you're ready, imagine your heart as the radiant sun at your chest's center, illuminating your entire being with its warmth and light. With each breath, sense your heart expanding, becoming a source of radiant love.
5. Let this love and light permeate every cell of your body, infusing them with warmth and brightness.
6. Now, expand this love and light beyond yourself and fill the room with it.
7. Extend this feeling to your loved ones, one by one, and then expand it out to envelop the whole Earth.
8. Bring your awareness back to your heart and bask in its glowing light; stay within its glow for as long as you please.

9. When you're ready, return to your breath and slowly open your eyes to complete the practice.

There are plenty of ways to extend this exercise. For instance:

- Focus your awareness on the sensation in the center of your heart. Allow it to guide you to a word or phrase to meditate on, and let that word or phrase permeate your being.
- Send love and compassion outward from your heart, directing it to whomever you choose, even yourself.
- Focus on the people whose love and understanding you want to receive, and let your heart fully receive their love.
- Before taking any action or making plans, reflect on your purpose and intention from your heart's center. Feel the sensation as your heartfelt intention permeates. This intention carries a distinct feeling. Keep this feeling with you as you go about doing your tasks.

Changing your life begins with changing your heart. Just as the sun sustains life, our heart's energy can create a beautiful and meaningful existence for ourselves and those around us.

Joy Hardy's poem serves as a powerful reminder of this truth:

The heart is a smaller cousin of the sun.

It sees and knows everything.
It hears the gnashing even as it hears the blessing.
The door to the mind should only be opened from the heart.
The enemy who gets in risks the danger of becoming a friend.

7. BONUS PRACTICE

Do you want something else to practice? If yes, I invite you to embrace contemplative practice as a way of finding rest from the constant rush of searching for answers.

In a world that favors quick solutions, contemplation calls for a pause. It encourages us to sit with our questions, allowing them to unfold within our consciousness. By embracing uncertainty and releasing our need for immediate answers, we create space for subtle feelings and intuitions to guide us.

Contemplation goes beyond the pursuit of straightforward intellectual responses; it invites a deeper connection and understanding that can be felt or sensed intuitively. It is the practice of immersing ourselves in receptive awareness, enabling insights, wisdom, and a profound sense of knowing.

To begin, I encourage you to revisit the questions provided at the end of each chapter. Choose a chapter that resonates with you and select a question that sparks your curiosity and interest. Whether you're taking a leisurely walk or meditating quietly, use the question as an anchor for your intention and attention. Let it float in your awareness and observe the feelings and sensations that arise within you. Answers may surface as clear thoughts or intuitive feelings. Embrace the pause and subtle knowing that emerges. Dedicate time to simply be present with the question without pressuring yourself to find immediate answers.

Engaging in contemplation invites us to leave space for the unknown and relinquish our inclination to categorize and label everything. This openness expands our vision beyond surface perceptions, fostering a way of living and breathing from a deeper place—the Heart Space.

SUMMARY: QUALITIES OF THE HEART SPACE

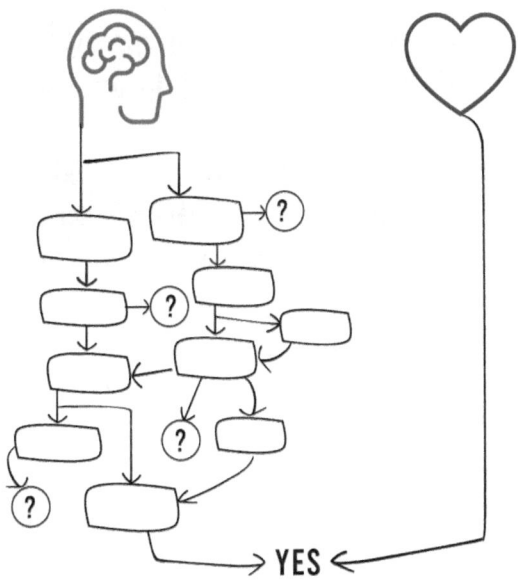

Inner knowing

In the Heart Space, there's an immediate knowing—a kind of understanding that happens right away without needing to think or reason. This quality goes beyond intellect and shows itself in an instant. It's direct, intuitive knowing that can't be put into words, a guiding force that communicates through feelings, nudges, and a sense of resonance with your truest selves. Within this sacred space, you tap into a rich source of wisdom. This helps you navigate life's complexities and gain a deeper understanding of your inner landscape. As this unfolds, your capacity for understanding and compassion grows toward others. It's liberating not to rely on our doubtful and limited minds to lead, but to work in harmony with the wisdom that comes from our hearts.

The Heart Space activates when you're willing to sense, feel, listen, and stay open. Here are its qualities:

- **Experiential:** understands reality through genuine encounters, fully immersing oneself in the moment and connections. It emphasizes "being with" rather than "being apart."
- **Reflective:** seeks to grasp the essence of oneself and the world, prioritizing "knowing through" rather than "knowing about."
- **Peripheral/Open Focus:** Emphasizes a wide and open awareness, allowing for a broader context and perspective.
- **Generative:** has the capacity to stimulate creativity, inspiration, and intuition by remaining open to new ideas and possibilities.

SUMMARY: QUALITIES OF THE HEART SPACE

- **Makes Room for Diversity:** utilizes diverse perspectives to form a comprehensive and holistic understanding of reality.
- **Observatory:** observes without forming judgments about what is being seen.
- **Embraces the Unknown:** comfortable without definite answers and remains open to different ideas, even when feels uncertain.
- **Connection-Based:** naturally pursues connections, interdependence, and deeper interactions, going beyond just surface-level engagements.
- **Spacious:** provides ample room to hold diverse emotions and movements without feeling constrained or crowded; prefers "Yes, and" over "No, but."
- **Integrative:** seeks harmony and resonance from diverse elements to form a unified whole.
- **Intuitive:** has the capacity to immediately sense or comprehend something, piercing through complexity and relying on wisdom and inner guidance rather than on reasoning or evidence.
- **Thrives in Trust:** blossoms and expands where there is trust and acceptance, allowing us to feel safe, supported, and free to be ourselves.
- **Seeks Understanding:** nurtures curiosity, openness, and a desire to understand oneself, others, and the world.

EPILOGUE

Your task is not to seek for love, but merely to seek and find all the barriers within yourself that you have built against it.

RUMI

Once we were invited to a Christmas dinner party at our friend's house. During the party, my five-year-old son received some Christmas gifts. He was delighted to unwrap them the next day.

The following morning, out of the blue, I heard my son crying. I rushed to him and asked, "What's wrong?"

"My Christmas gifts are gone! I can't find them!" he said, trying to catch his breath. He was devastated.

I was sure we had brought them home the night before. But to make sure, I asked him, "Did you carry them home?"

He said, still with tears, "Yes, I saw Daddy carry them in a bag with him."

I felt relieved and said, "Well, if you can't find them, it

doesn't mean you've lost them. Your Christmas gifts are here somewhere. Why don't you look for them again?"

Five minutes later, he found what he was looking for.

What happened to my son reminds me of what has happened to all of us. We often frantically look for things we think are missing, forgetting they are actually present in our lives. Just because we can't see them doesn't mean they're gone.

Our lives are like a house with many rooms, each filled with unique gifts. Though we are often conditioned to believe that growth, fulfillment, and happiness lie outside of ourselves, the truth is that everything we need and want already exists within us. They may not be visible to our eyes yet, but that's not because they aren't there. We must open our hearts and look within.

Instead of getting stuck in our heads and feeling like we have nothing or lost something, the Heart Space helps us remember that the answers and solutions to our problems are just in the next room over. We can rest easy, knowing that all we need is within our reach. This trust is the antidote to our survival mind.

Safety isn't about knowing all the answers or ensuring everything is in order; it's a deep understanding that all is well no matter what happens. To experience this truth, we need a holistic way of seeing, a deeper sense of who we are beyond our physical bodies, and the realization that we are not alone. Such awareness can bring inner peace and contentment that surpasses intellectual understanding.

When we feel safe and secure, our survival mind no longer dominates our actions. We are free to use our attention and intention for the greater good. With our minds at peace, we can tap into the wisdom and intuition that come from a deeper knowing beyond conscious reasoning. By integrating our mental faculties, we ensure that our capacity to think and reason supports us instead of working against us.

I believe our journey to the heart is a voyage to discover what it means to be human. It's about treasuring the full spectrum of our differences, stories, and experiences. Without the ups and downs, varying perspectives, and opinions, conversations lose depth, discussions lack engagement, and the chance to learn from each other fades. In these experiences, we encounter newness, are caught by surprise, struck by profound insights, and moved by moments of gratitude. We can find joy amidst sadness, pleasure in the midst of pain, peace within turmoil, and unity despite disparities. Through it all, we're given the opportunity to love, be kind, show compassion, and forgive—not out of obligation, but because we embrace the freedom to do so.

Our journey to the heart is a continuous practice of expanding and deepening our understanding of our inner workings and what makes us free. It liberates us from fear, not by pushing it away, but by acknowledging and understanding our vulnerabilities. When we do this, we can give and experience greater compassion, love, and understanding, for we can only love when we're free to be ourselves. Such knowledge cannot be attained by logical reasoning alone but only through the direct experience of becoming love itself.

The journey of the heart is relevant in all domains of our lives, including business, politics, economy, education, and technology. This is because no matter which domain we explore, it all comes back to being human—we are at the center of it all. And it all must start with loving ourselves. Our task isn't to change the world, but to intimately know ourselves, for the essence of the world resides within each of us. As we evolve, so does the world around us. In this era of uncertainty, as old structures crumble and new ones emerge, we can cultivate a greater capacity to endure discomfort and learn the art of living with possibilities.

Welcome to the era of the heart. Let's begin together.

AFTERWORD

Thank you for purchasing and reading my book. I hope you find it useful and that it resonates with you in a meaningful way. Now that you've completed the journey, I'm excited to invite you to explore further with me! Visit my website at **www.christinesamuel.ca** to join the Heart Space community, discover upcoming events, access more content, and stay connected with me.

If you found my book helpful, I'd love it if you could share it with your friends and family. Leaving a review on Amazon or your social media would be amazing! This will help raise awareness about living from the Heart Space so others can benefit too.

Thank you for being a part of this journey. I look forward to connecting with you in the future.

END NOTES

CHAPTER 1

Hutchins, Giles and Laura Storm. *Regenerative Leadership: The DNA of Life-Affirming 21st Century Organizations.* Royal Tunbridge Wells: Wordzworth, 2019.

"Bacon, Francis." In *Stanford Encyclopedia of Philosophy*, ed. Edward N. Zalta, https://plato.stanford.edu/entries/francis-bacon/.

Spencer, J. Brooke, Stephen G. Brush, Margaret J. Osler, Adam Augustyn, Erik Gregersen, and Melissa Petruzzello. "Scientific Revolution." In Encyclopædia Britannica. https://www.britannica.com/science/Scientific-Revolution.

Newman, Lex. "Descartes' Epistemology." In Stanford Encyclopedia of Philosophy, ed. Edward N. Zalta. https://plato.stanford.edu/entries/descartes-epistemology/.

Suzuki, David. *The Sacred Balance: Rediscovering Our Place in Nature.* 3rd ed. Vancouver, CA: Greystone Books, 2007.

Watts, Alan. *The Wisdom of Insecurity: A Message for an Age of Anxiety.* New York: Vintage, 2011.

Helminski, Kabir Edmund. *Living Presence: The Sufi Path to Mindfulness and the Essential Self.* New York: TarcherPerigee, 2017.

Feldenkrais, Moshe. *Body and Mature Behavior: A Study of Anxiety, Sex, Gravitation, and Learning.* Berkeley: Frog Books, 2005.

CHAPTER 2

Harper, Douglas. "Success."In *Online Etymology Dictionary.* https://www.etymonline.com/word/success.

Lotto, Beau. *Deviate: The Science of Seeing Differently.* New York: Hachette Books, 2019.

Seth, Anil. "The hard problem of consciousness is a distraction from the real one."*Aeon.* https://aeon.co/essays/the-hard-problem-of-consciousness-is-a-distraction-from-the-real-one.

Pillay, Srini. "Challenging Old Theories About the Brain—and Spirit." Collective Trauma Summit 2019, Day 6.

Williamson, Marianne. *A Return to Love*. San Franscico: HarperOne, 1992.

Weizmann Institute of Science."Quantum Mechanics."ScienceDaily. https://www.sciencedaily.com/releases/1998/02/980227055013.htm.

Steve Jobs. "Steve Jobs Secrets of Life."2011, YouTube video. https://www.youtube.com/watch?v=kYfNvmF0Bqw.

CHAPTER 3

Porges, Stephen W. *The Pocket Guide to the Polyvagal Theory: The Transformative Power of Feeling Safe*. Illustrated ed. New York: WW Norton, 2017.

Stewart, Matthew. *The 9.9 Percent: The New Aristocracy That Is Entrenching Inequality and Warping Our Culture*. New York: Simon and Schuster, 2021.

Stewart, Emily. "The problem with America's semi-rich."*Vox*, October 12, 2021, https://www.vox.com/the-goods/22673605/upper-middle-class-meritocracy-matthew-stewart.

CHAPTER 4

Rohr, Richard. *The Naked Now: Learning to See as the Mystics See*. New York: The Crossroad Publishing Company, 2009.

Wikipedia contributors. "Attention schema theory." Wikipedia, last modified June 12, 2023, https://en.wikipedia.org/wiki/Attention_schema_theory.

Wilterson, Andrew I., Casey M. Kemper, Noah Kim, Taylor W. Webb, Alexandra M.W. Reblando, and Michael S.A. Graziano. "Attention Control and the Attention Schema Theory of Consciousness." *Progress in Neurobiology 195*(2020).https://doi.org/10.1016/j.pneurobio.2020.101844.

Hoffman, Donald. "Do we see reality as it is?" YouTube video, posted by TED, February 7, 2017. https://www.youtube.com/watch?v=oYp5XuGYqqY.

Rohr, Richard. *Falling Upward: A Spirituality for the Two Halves of Life*. San Francisco: Jossey-Bass, 2011.

Nhat Hanh, Thich. *How to Love*. Illustrated ed. Berkeley: Parallax Press, 2014.

SECTION TWO: THE HEART SPACE INTRODUCTION

Anderson, Micheline. "The Spiritual Heart." *Religions 11* (2020): 506. doi:10.3390/rel11100506.

Slote, Michael. "Yin-Yang, Mind, and Heart-Mind."In *Between Psychology and Philosophy, Palgrave Studies in Comparative East-West Philosophy.* Palgrave Macmillan, Cham, 2020. https://doi.org/10.1007/978-3-030-22503-2_2.

McCraty, Rollin, Ph.D. *Science of the Heart: Exploring the Role of the Heart in Human Performance Volume 2.* Boulder Creek, CA: HeartMath Institute, 2015.

Festival of Faiths. "'Being' Is Not Something You Are . . . with Cynthia Bourgealt." YouTube video, May 20, 2019. https://www.youtube.com/watch?v=5ALAgUlzxX0&t=386s.

CHAPTER 5

Van Morrison. "*I Forgot That Love Existed.*" YouTube video, 3:23. Posted by Van Morrison Official, December 4, 2015. https://www.youtube.com/watch?v=SseS5ATB2wI.

O'Donohue, John. *Divine Beauty: The Invisible Embrace.* New York: Bantam, 2003.

Rohr, Richard. *The Naked Now: Learning to See as the Mystics See.* Crossroad, 2009.

Frankl, Viktor E. *Man's Search for Meaning.* Boston: Beacon Press, 2006.

Chödrön, Pema. *Start Where You Are: A Guide to Compassionate Living.* Boston: Shambhala Publications, 2018.

Keller, Helen. *The Story of My Life.* New York: Doubleday, Page & Company, 1903.

Sardello, Robert. *Heartfulness.* Colorado: Goldenstone Press, 2017.

CHAPTER 6

Grant, Kathryn. "How Many Ancestors Do I Have?" (And Other Fun Questions to Help You Connect with Family). Blog post. FamilySearch,

December 2, 2022. https://www.familysearch.org/en/blog/how-many-ancestors-do-i-have.

Dawe, Gavin S., Xing Wei Tan, and Zhi-Cheng Xiao. "Cell migration from baby to mother." *Cell Adhesion & Migration 1*, no. 1 (2007): 19-27. https://www.ncbi.nlm.nih.gov/pmc/articles/PMC2633676/.

"Microbial Dimension to Human Development and Well-Being." In *The Convergence of Infectious Diseases and Noncommunicable Diseases: Proceedings of a Workshop*. Eds. Allen Nicholson, Yenew Kebede Negussie, Carlos M. Shah, et al. Washington, DC: National Academies Press, 2019. https://www.ncbi.nlm.nih.gov/books/NBK552459/.

Davey, Reginald. "What Chemical Elements are Found in the Human Body?" News-Medical.net. https://www.news-medical.net/life-sciences/What-Chemical-Elements-are-Found-in-the-Human-Body.aspx.

Haines, Arthur. "Why I'm Learning an Indigenous Language." Arthur Haines, June 13, 2014. http://www.arthurhaines.com/blog/2014/6/13/why-im-learning-an-indigenous-language.

Kimmerer, Robin Wall. *Braiding Sweetgrass: Indigenous Wisdom, Scientific Knowledge, and the Teachings of Plants*. Minneapolis: Milkweed Editions, 2013.

Tayag, Yasmin. "Six NASA Astronauts Describe the Moment in Space When 'Everything Changed.'" *Inverse*. March 27, 2018. https://www.inverse.com/article/42902-nasa-astronauts-describe-overview-effect-everything-changed.

Herman, Rhett. "How Fast Is the Earth Moving?" *Scientific American*. October 26, 1998. https://www.scientificamerican.com/article/how-fast-is-the-earth-mov/.

CHAPTER 7

Varty, Boyd. *The Lion Tracker's Guide to Life*. New York: Random House, 2020.

Ferriss, Tim. "Boyed Varty Transcript." The Tim Ferriss Show. February 18, 2022. https://tim.blog/2022/02/18/boyd-varty-transcript/.

Matousek, Mark. *Writing to Awaken: A Journey of Truth, Transformation, and Self-Discovery*.Oakland, CA: Reveal Press, 2017.

CHAPTER 8

Kanazawa, Kenichi. "Corona on a Steel Plate." YouTube video, Posted by Kenichi Kanazawa, May 15, 2020. https://www.youtube.com/watch?v=qxdJ-ebNi14&t=120s.

"Hans Jenny and the Science of Sound: Cymatics." *Geometry Matters.* August 11, 2021. https://geometrymatters.com/hans-jenny-and-the-science-of-sound-cymatics/.

Matthew 6:34. New American Standard Bible.

Helminski, Kabir. *Living Presence: A Sufi Way to Mindfulness & the Essential Self.* New York: Jeremy P. Tarcher/Putnam, 1992.

Mate, Gabor. "Can People Ever Really Change?" Instagram, September 16, 2022. https://www.instagram.com/p/CikxdV0gUsO/.

Watts, Mary S. *The Nature of Consciousness: Essays on the Unity of Mind and Matter.* Chicago: Theosophical Publishing House, 2017.

CHAPTER 9

Baeck, Ria. *Collective Presencing: An Emerging Human Capacity.* https://book.collectivepresencing.org/.

Monbiot, George. "The Secret World Beneath Our Feet Is Mind-Blowing." *The Guardian,* May 7, 2022. https://www.theguardian.com/environment/2022/may/07/secret-world-beneath-our-feet-mind-blowing-key-to-planets-future.

O'Donohue, John. *Conamara Blues: Poems.* New York: Harper Perennial, 2001.

Helminski, Kabir. *Living Presence: A Sufi Way to Mindfulness & the Essential Self.* New York: Jeremy P. Tarcher/Putnam, 1992.

Houston, Pam. "Toni Morrison: The Precious Moments a Writer Lives For." *Oprah Magazine.* July, 2009. https://www.oprah.com/omagazine/toni-morrison-on-writing/all.

Gibran, Khalil. *The Prophet.* New York: Alfred A. Knopf, 1923.

Rohr, Richard. *The Naked Now: Learning to See as the Mystics See.* New York: The Crossroad Publishing Company, 2009.

Nhat Hanh, Thich. *The Heart of Understanding: Commentaries on the Prajnaparamita Heart Sutra.* Berkeley, CA: Parallax Press, 1988.

CHAPTER 10

Liu, Eric, and Scott Noppe-Brandon. *Imagination First: Unlocking the Power of Possibility*. San Francisco: Jossey-Bass, April 26, 2011.

Tippett, Krista. "Pico Iyer—The Urgency of Slowing Down," *On Being with Krista Tippett*, June 4, 2015. https://onbeing.org/programs/pico-iyer-the-urgency-of-slowing-down-nov2018/.

Wisdom Keepers, "Wiruungga Dunggiirr," TikTok, August 18, 2022. https://www.tiktok.com/@wisdom.keepers/video/7133135408946253061?lang=en.

"Intend," Collins Dictionary, Collins, https://www.collinsdictionary.com/dictionary/english/intend.

Harjo, Joy, *Conflict Resolution for Holy Beings: Poems*. New York: W. W. Norton & Company, 2015.

ABOUT THE AUTHOR

Christine Samuel firmly believes that in this era of Artificial Intelligence, humanity must provide values that technology cannot—by becoming more human. With over 20 years of experience in the User Experience field, bridging the interaction between humans and technology, she now dedicates her life to sharing her lifetime observations, insights, and extensive research in creating transformative human experiences. Her mission is to explore how we can bring Relational Intelligence into the way we work together.

Christine actively supports individuals and organizations in navigating their transitions in a rapidly changing world. Through coaching, facilitation, and speaking engagements, she assists them in cultivating deep listening skills, self-awareness, and heart-centered wisdom.

She resides in Toronto with her husband, two children, a cat and a dog.

Connect with her at www.ChristineSamuel.ca.

www.ingramcontent.com/pod-product-compliance
Lightning Source LLC
Chambersburg PA
CBHW060601080526
44585CB00013B/646